I0685427

APPALACHIAN
REVIEW

VOL. 50, NO. 4
FALL 2022

TRADITION. DIVERSITY. CHANGE.

EDITOR
Jason Kyle Howard

BOOK REVIEWS EDITOR
Emily Masters

STUDENT ASSISTANTS
Lie Ford
Soul Nwaokoro
Ian Williamson

MANUSCRIPT READERS
Katherine Scott Crawford
Patti Frye Meredith

ADVISORY BOARD

Richard Hague
Marc Harshman
Maurice Manning
Karen Salyer McElmurray

Lee Smith
Lyrae Van Clief-Stefanon
Neela Vaswani
Crystal Wilkinson

ESTABLISHED IN 1973
PUBLISHED QUARTERLY
by Berea College
www.appalachianreview.net

©2022 by Berea College. Vol. 50, No. 4, Fall 2022. All rights reserved. No part of this publication may be reproduced without the prior permission of *Appalachian Review*. Periodicals postage paid at Berea, Kentucky, and at additional mailing offices. ISSN# 2692-9244 (Print); ISSN# 2692-9287 (Digital).

The short stories in this publication are works of fiction. Names, characters, places, and incidents are either the products of the authors' imaginations or are used fictitiously. Any resemblance to actual events, locales, or persons, living or dead, is entirely coincidental. The views expressed in the creative nonfiction herein are solely those of the authors.

Electronic submissions only at www.appalachianreview.net. Distributed through a partnership between the University of North Carolina Press and Duke University Press. Basic subscription price: $32/year for individuals, $62/year for institutions. For subscription requests and inquiries, visit the magazine's website, email subscriptions@dukeupress.edu, or call 888-651-0122 (toll-free in the US and Canada) or 919-688-5134.

CONTENTS

EDITOR'S NOTE.........................*Jason Kyle Howard*   5

FICTION
Dinamarie Isola
    The Pact...   8

CREATIVE NONFICTION
Dan Leach
    Challenger...   26
Melissa Helton
    Day Seven..   78
Kirsten Reneau
    On Grafton, West Virginia in the Fall   88

POETRY
Lynn Gilbert
    Wind Chill   24
    Theft   25
Hayley Phillips
    Godpained   53
    Séance   54
Adam Day
    Intervention   73
    Playing a Part..   74
    Passing Storefronts   75
    Thirsty Heat...   76
    Wood Thrushes..   77

Gabriel Dunsmith
    Auguring a Midnight Field 86
Elan Maier
    Baseball 87
Rachel Bates
    Remembering Pandemic Teaching 102
    Divorcée Dating 103
Addison Griffis
    Month-End Ritual on Mississippi Title Application 108
    Business Tool on Odometer Statement 109

INTERVIEW
Jason Kyle Howard
    Erin Keane 55

CRAFT ESSAY
Jake Maynard
    Fictive Dreamin' 91

BOOK REVIEWS
Randi Adams
    The Poison Flood by Jordan Farmer 104

CONTRIBUTORS
CONTRIBUTORS 110

COVER PHOTOGRAPH
Castiglione del Lago lights by Diz Play

EDITOR'S NOTE

JASON KYLE HOWARD

I t's been a week," Melissa Helton's essay "Day Seven" begins. "And I don't know what to say. It is so big."

In the essay, Helton, a writer and staffer at the Hindman Settlement School, recounts the aftermath of the late July floods that left forty-four dead, thousands of homes damaged or destroyed, and hundreds displaced throughout eastern

Kentucky. The offices and some lodging quarters at Hindman were destroyed, and its archives—a repository of Appalachian culture that housed valuable, important materials about the school's founding and rare books from the library of author James Still—were devastated. For months, Helton coordinated an effort to salvage materials from the archives, as well as relief efforts that distributed food, clothing, cleaning supplies, and personal goods to individuals around Hindman that were affected by the flooding.

"Day Seven" is a gripping account of the communal and personal aftermath, capturing the emotional whiplash that Helton, and hundreds of others like her, experienced. But it also reflects something more: the finest qualities of the region and its residents.

This issue contains other insights into the region. In her short story "The Pact," Dinamarie Isola writes of a mother struggling to take the high road after a divorce for the sake of her child. Dan Leach's memorable essay "Challenger" captures the anxieties of a twelve-year-old narrator surrounding the Y2K bug, divorce, and school. Kirsten Reneau pays tribute to West Virginia and James Agee in her lyric essay "On Grafton, West Virginia in the Fall." Poets Adam Day, Gabriel Dunsmith, Rachel Bates, and others offer resonant images and verse rooted in the natural world, the pandemic, and romance.

We're also pleased to feature a conversation with *Appalachian Review* contributor and *Salon* editor-in-chief Erin Keane, whose recent essay collection *Runaway: Notes on the Myths That Made Me* was published in September to widespread critical buzz. Frequent contributor Jake Maynard offers his insights about the connection between dream life and the writing process in "Fictive Dreamin'," an engaging craft essay.

Flood relief efforts continue in eastern Kentucky, so please consider making a contribution if you are in a position to do so. Hindman Settlement School suffered substantial damage and has provided essential housing and relief to hundreds in surrounding communities. The offices and archives at Appalshop, which has been a cultural mainstay for decades, faced devastation. Eastern Kentucky Mutual Aid immediately began fundraising efforts for flooding victims. Kentucky Governor Andy Beshear has announced a relief fund that will distribute aid to impacted individuals, families, and communities.

As Helton writes, "We are a community that says we are blessed even as we stand amidst destruction and loss and fear...that we are just happy to be able to help." ∎

THE PACT

DINAMARIE ISOLA

Lara shuffles college brochures like she's a blackjack dealer. Glossy and slick, they slide through her hands every time the car shifts gears as we climb the winding back roads. Tightening my grip on the steering wheel does little to ease the rocking and shaking. The force reverberates from my insides, out to my trembling fingers.

The same question plays in my head: *Is she ready to launch or at least perch on the ledge of her father's life? Can I turn her over to Roy and his crusty mother, Adeline?*

I steal a sideways glance, like that will buy us five more minutes, when I really want five more years. When I think of a home without her present, the tears well up.

"How am I supposed to decide?" Lara asks.

I release a breath. "You'll know when you know." *Or you'll learn to live with your decision.* I quickly usher that errant thought out like a trash can of dead fish. "And if it turns out to be the wrong choice, leaving is always an option."

"Kind of like your philosophy for falling in love?" Her squinty eyes and twisted mouth are proof that she pays more attention than I give her credit for.

I've never given her the details leading up to the divorce for fear of facing her disgust. I stayed a decade too long with a man whose love affair with whiskey was more passionate than anything he felt for me or the other women he bedded. The ones who left his clothes smudged with spray tan, his skin glistening like a disco ball.

For now, the southern sun warms her and casts a gentle glow on her father. Lara doesn't dwell on the fact that Roy chose to move back to South Carolina, instead of staying in New York to be near her. In fact, his residency might save the day if she attends Clemson University and can qualify for the in-state tuition rate. And isn't that just like Roy to get all the glory without working at it, like me. He hasn't had to sit through soccer tournaments in the rain, and trips to the ER for x-rays. The college searches, essay writing, and the school visits—all carefully mapped out to avoid missing her soccer obligations—everything managed by me. All so I can turn her over to him?

After miles of monotonous driving on dirt roads, I turn in to the mouth of Adeline's driveway. Shrouded by unruly brush, the wild branches strain to clutch at us.

Nature shouldn't be so ugly.

I hold my breath, stomping on the gas pedal to blow through the quarter-mile tunnel of dreary greenery. And as we come out on the other side, into the pebbled clearing, I release my breath, but it catches it when Roy leaps off the sagging front porch. He lands with a thud, kicking up dust from his boots.

I cut the wheel and force myself not to spin us fully around, back down the driveway. Instead, I coast, prepared to pull over and park. Lara rolls down her window, waving with an enthusiasm she hasn't possessed since grade school. A fleeting, rare moment, and Roy gets to bask in it, unaware of how precious it is.

Trotting alongside the car, he reaches in and grabs Lara's hand. He puts on a show, flapping his arms like a windmill, huffing, pretending that he can't keep up. And Lara indulges him by throwing back her head, laughing wildly. He is the funniest man alive. If I tried something playful like that, she would tell me that I was embarrassing her.

"Dad!" she shrieks. Tears trickle down the side of her face.

"I've got you, darlin'," he pants.

I pull up behind a red pickup and shift into park to kill this game. But Roy keeps playing. He doubles over and drops his right hand to his chest. Still holding on to Lara with his left, he raises both of their hands higher.

"Told you I wouldn't let you go."

I suppose the past two years don't count.

He yanks open the door, and Lara busts out like being near me one more second might kill her. I climb from the car and stand useless, watching Lara squeal as Roy spins her in an air hug. That sound hasn't come out of her in years, not around me, at least. I want to be happy for her, so I push down the salt gathering in the back of my throat and steel myself for high alert. My role as protector hasn't changed because she believes she's an adult. Roy might seem like he's harmless fun, but I know better. It has taken me years to repair my heart and my credit score.

"Mama made lunch. You hungry?" Roy's first words to me are nothing but a reminder that the only woman he clings to is Mama Adeline.

"I'm starving!" Lara answers, thinking every question is for her.

"Beth?"

My eyes itch just looking at him. Only three years older than I am, he looks weathered by over a decade; his crow's-feet deep as coin slots. Tired smile, dull eyes, he's lost the sparkle that was bright enough to make the most homely or boring person feel special.

"Beth?" With his head tilted to the ground and his eyes raised, he peeks at me through his hair, like a sorry dog who ate the Sunday roast beef.

Lara glares at me. "Aren't you going to say hello?"

He hasn't said hello, either. But there are never free passes for me. She saves them all for him.

"Hi." I nod and raise my palm in a flat wave.

"Aw, come on, now! Don't be so New York cool." Roy slides his hand around my waist and yanks me in for a hug. He folds his body around mine as if we've never been apart, and the familiarity of it all, right down to his aftershave, makes my spine tighten like it might snap. He doesn't get to have any more of me. I pat his shoulder much like a wrestler taps out. And as I push away, Lara shakes her head and stomps her foot once.

What does she expect from me? I've been alone with her, no help from him—money or otherwise—for nearly two years.

Truthfully, long before he left, I was on my own. And while I don't want her to hate Roy, her enthusiasm for him leaves me feeling barely tolerated. A stupid, irrational thought creeps in, wishing there were a younger child to devote myself to, to make me feel like I matter again after Lara leaves. A child who would understand that good parenting requires being present, not putting on a show.

Adeline's arrival on the porch is announced with the slap of the screen door. My ex-mother-in-law stands like a harmless flamingo on thin, delicate legs, cranes her neck, and squints. Her limited eyesight is the only sign that she's a few years older than when I last saw her; unlike her son.

"Lara?" Adeline calls, her voice dripping with Southern syrup. "Look at you, girl, all grown up!"

Lara hops on to the porch and embraces her grandmother. Adeline hugs her back and, over my daughter's shoulder, gives me a fleeting glance served with a side of serrated silence.

A stupid, irrational thought creeps in, wishing there were a younger child to devote myself to, to make me feel like I matter again after Lara leaves.

I plant my feet and fold my arms. Adeline never liked me, and she can continue to hate me all she wants. Weeks away from turning eighteen, Lara can decide the place Roy and Adeline will have in her life, and she will arrange any future visits on her own. This is my last family reunion.

"You must be starving," Roy says; Adeline shoots him a look that freezes him in place.

"Actually, I need to use the bathroom," I say.

As he trails after me, Adeline snaps, "She knows where the bathroom is, son."

Open-mouthed, Roy twists his neck between me and his mother, like he wants to cross a highway on foot and is afraid of becoming roadkill. I shake my head and smile. She can have him.

I yank the screen door open, and it slams loudly behind me. From outside, Adeline starts what she is good at—running commentary fueled with bitterness.

"Well, she's in a huff," Adeline squawks.

"Mama, you know as well as I do that the door shuts quickly."

"Yes'm, it most certainly does."

In some circles the faded turquoise Formica countertops and dull farmhouse sink would be considered shabby chic. But here, it's pure dinge. The wooden table Roy's father, Amos, made held up the best. I imagine Roy oiling it regularly for fear that Amos' ghost will come back and continue the beatings where they left off.

In the center of the table sits a sweating pitcher of tea, with hunks of lemon brightening the murky brown liquid. A blue-checkered cloth napkin cinched with a wooden ring sits in the middle of each of the three plates. *Three.*

I was going to check in to the motel while Lara visited. But Adeline's desire to steer this visit is a claw on my neck. Why should she get her way? Yet, it's complicated. There is no winning with Adeline. If she gets me to run off to the motel, she has control. If I stay and I lose my temper at some insult she is bound to hurl at me, she'll get to say, *See, I told you she's a no-good, stuck-up Yankee bitch.*

She married an abusive alcoholic and lived out her marriage like a prison sentence, freed only by Amos' death. She expected the same of me, especially since her son's abuse never left me bruised and battered.

"We don't do divorce in our family. That's a sin against God," she chided me once we announced our split.

"Adultery isn't?" I shot back.

"That's the sign of a woman who can't make her man happy."

"That's like saying a woman deserves her beatings."

Adeline gave a stunned, slow blink and said, "He's better off without you. You and your fresh mouth."

"Because he's such a prize," I muttered.

Lara's shocked laughter wafts through the screen door to punch my gut. "Grandma!"

I try not to imagine the jabs being made at my expense, my daughter's giggles fueling Adeline's nasty impulses. As I start off for the bathroom, I catch myself.

Don't make her happy.

The silverware drawer sticks, and I hold my breath while I shimmy it open. I pluck a fork, knife, and napkin ring. From her linen drawer I get a yellowing white cloth napkin; there aren't any more with the blue-checkered pattern. I take a plate and glass from the thick wooden shelf over the sink, careful not to ping them. Once my place is set, I head to the bathroom. And when I emerge, Roy is waiting, leaning against the kitchen counter.

"You find everything okay?" His lopsided grin used to make my stomach flip around with hot swirls. Now, his charm feels like illusion, a cheap show.

"Bathroom's still in the same place."

The corners of his mouth droop, the smile melting off his face.

"Lara, she's just…so grown-up, so beautiful." Thick with emotion, he finally seems regretful of cheating his daughter of time she'll never get back.

"She has a big future ahead of her. Lots of decisions." I sound like her college counselor and not her mother, because Roy needs to understand Lara's college search is the only reason I'm here. This isn't old homecoming week.

"Do you think she'll really go to Clemson? That must be killing you." He laughs.

Her leaving is difficult enough. Choosing Roy's alma mater and, worse, moving in with him feels like a hot backhand to my face.

"She's had some great offers in New York too. It would be more affordable and closer to home. We'll see."

"I can't imagine that in-state tuition at Clemson will be more expensive than New York schools."

"Certainly more convenient if she stayed in New York," I say, my voice trembling. *Please,* I want to say, *please tell her you can't help her.* And this time, when my gut clenches, it's on account of my selfishness. Lara won't tell me for certain, but Clemson is her top pick.

He stares at me, his eyes softening. "I'm sorry if I made you sad," he whispers. "I never meant to hurt you."

"It's Lara you should be saying this to. I've long given up on feeling hurt. You moved away from her and haven't been part of her life in years." The crack in my voice says otherwise.

"We talk on the phone," he whines. "I'm here for her. I'm not going anywhere."

Indeed.

A familiar rage bubbles in me. I chose him to be her father. I knew a baby would never change him, yet still, I gambled with her life the moment I tried to conceive. Even if he wanted to, he was incapable of putting a child first. He didn't value his own life; how could I have expected him to treasure hers? And now that he's able to make things right with her, I don't want him to—just so I can keep her near me.

"Well, let her know that, because if she picks Clemson, the only way this works is if you're sober and she stays with you. Can you do that?" I glare at him, challenging him to give me a

15

sign that he's not fit. But instead of smiling and brushing over it, his eyes brim with tears.

"I promise. I know I have a lot to make up to her. To both of you." He blinks and looks away. I'm not sure who is more stunned by his honest admission.

The zipping sound of air moving through the screen door is the period on the end of this conversation. Adeline totters in, her head jerking like a mother duck in search of an errant duckling. As Roy wipes his face on his sleeve, her mouth twists, and her eyes stab at mine. Lara's eyes widen at the sight of her father's blotchy face, and she shoots me an accusatory glare, like I'm responsible for all that ails Roy.

"That's some truck out there," I say, searching for a harmless topic.

His face brightens, until Adeline starts in. "It's not new like your car. He bought it cheap and put a lot of work into it. It's not worth much."

I shrug. I don't know much about trucks, or their value. But I do know how she thinks. She's worried I'm coming after whatever assets he has. I waived my rights to anything of Roy's when we divorced; besides, a used truck can't settle us up. No, being there for Lara is how he can make good.

"Well, you did a nice job," I tell him. It's the truth, but it also elicits a huff from Adeline, who stares at the extra place setting and scowls at Roy. I smile and let her think that he overrode her slight and made room for me at the table.

"Is that iced tea?" Lara says, grabbing the pitcher and pouring a glass. Adeline shoots her a look, like Lara opened the refrigerator without asking.

"I'd like some too, if it's not too much trouble." The sharpness in Adeline's voice causes Lara to tilt her head.

"Sure, Grandma. Is everyone having?" Lara doesn't wait for us to answer; she fills three glasses.

Roy looks at the floor. "You know, there's no need to stay at the motel. We have plenty of room," he says. "I can sleep on the couch, and you two can have my room."

Before I can refuse him, Lara gives an enthusiastic *great* just as Adeline whispers loudly, "Now, we talked about this already, son." Tight, her mouth looks like a beak ready to peck out his eyes.

Watching my daughter's face fall, I push my nails into the palm of my hand to remind myself not to give Adeline a reaction.

"I'll be more comfortable at the motel, but thanks. She can stay here." Lara's chin quivers, and she sips her tea, and my stomach turns. *Did she expect a romantic reunion?*

"You can sleep with me, sugar." Adeline's voice is sweet as honey.

Lara guzzles her iced tea as if that will cool the red splotches crawling up her neck. Embarrassment, anger—it's hard to tell what she's thinking.

"Hey, we forgot the gifts," I say. "Come to the car with me?"

She nods and follows. The thwacking sound of the screen door is like a karate chop to my neck.

"Honey, are you okay?" I say once we're at the car.

"I'm fine." Her high-pitched tone is the same one she gives me when she wants to freeze me out.

I pop the trunk and dig out the two gift bags that Lara put together. She snatches the bags from my hands.

"Why are you so upset?" I reach to brush away a stray hair from her face, but she backs away.

"I'm not. God! Just stop talking; you're so annoying." She rolls her eyes, and I take my hurt out on the trunk, slamming it with a force that vibrates up my arms. We trudge back up to the porch. I keep quiet because anything I say will travel into the house. Adeline would like nothing more than to hear us fight.

Lara's mood brightens as we enter to find Roy pulling out a plate of fried chicken from the refrigerator.

"No, that's for another time," Adeline snaps. "Grab the cold cuts and the potato salad."

"But she loves fried chicken. We all do," he pleads, but his mother shakes her head, and he reaches back into the refrigerator to switch out the plates.

"Here you go," Lara says, handing the yellow bag to Roy and the green one to Adeline.

Roy gives an embarrassed smile. It wouldn't occur to him to have a little something for his daughter, and my heart sinks for her. Adeline didn't think to do anything, either. And the one thing she can do—the stupid fried chicken— she won't because she knows I like it too. She'd rather win than do the right thing. Hurting me is more important than enjoying Lara.

Adeline takes a box out of the bag and opens it, pulling out the coffee mug. She squints.

"Don't you like it?" Lara asks.

"What is this supposed to be?" Adeline turns the mug; it is the one intended for my father, a picture of him dancing with Lara at the father-daughter dance. "Is this some kind of a dig?"

"Now why would she do that? It's a mix-up, plain and simple." Roy opens his mug to find Lara's class picture on it. "Beautiful, sweetheart. Every time I use it, I'll think of you." Her face goes blank as he gives her arm a squeeze.

"What am I to do with this?" Adeline thrusts the mug back at Lara, who is too stunned to react.

I reach out and tear it from Adeline's grip while Lara looks on. *Don't give her what she wants.*

"'Thank you for thinking of me' would do nicely." Hands shaking, I pull the box out of her other hand and tuck the mug in.

Roy flops down with a sigh and starts to put potato salad on his plate. Whenever he doesn't want to deal with something stressful, he quietly fades away. How will he ever be able to look out for Lara?

My mistake was making excuses for him, lying to my daughter until she wasn't sure what was true. Any time Roy disappeared I told her he needed space to cool off. Because I didn't want her to know he couldn't get himself together; even for her, it seemed. But after a while I didn't know how to explain his absences. She accused me of not caring enough to make sure he was okay. By the last time he left, I would have paid for his plane ticket. I told him where he should go—to hell and to his

I told him where he should go—to hell and to his mother, because that was a twofer. It was the only time he ever listened. The truth is I gave him permission to leave his daughter.

mother, because that was a twofer. It was the only time he ever listened. The truth is I gave him permission to leave his daughter.

Lara sinks down next to him, like she needs a rest; but I can't sit. No matter what I do, Adeline is going to be happy. Where there is pain, she finds joy.

"I'm more tired than hungry. I think I'll head over to the motel and take a nap." Lara doesn't react and neither does Roy.

"Of course, you will," Adeline snorts. "You taking her with you?"

I look at Lara, but she's staring at her hands. Sitting like that, next to Roy, I worry that she's giving in to that pull, to dim her light just as Roy does in Adeline's presence.

"No. She's been looking forward to this visit for a long time now." I won't use my daughter as a weapon, even if that is the fastest way to make Adeline angry.

Adeline's face twists, like she's caught me in a lie. "I thought you were visiting fancy schools."

"She has some decisions to make. I wanted her to have another look."

"Expensive, aren't they?" She snorts. "You know he can't help you."

When has he ever? I look at Roy; his head hangs limply. "I don't recall having asked."

"What do you call living with us? I expect you'll pay us room and board, same as you would the school?" Adeline sniffs. "We got bills, same as you."

My eyes dart to Roy, who won't even look at me. This part he never covered with me or, judging by her wide eyes, Lara.

"Yes, I know all about bills, Adeline. Some, your son left me digging out from and then there's the pile I've been paying on my own for years."

"Not my fault you didn't ask for money from him." She clicks her gums, and my fist clenches.

"Mama…" Roy's warning crawls out of him, a weak beg.

"I don't want a thing from him, but it would sure be nice if he felt compelled to help his daughter for a change," I snap.

Eyes lowered, Lara chews her lip and shakes her head. Her silence as good as her screaming *Stop!*

If only she could see the pain in my eyes, maybe she would understand my worry. Roy is incapable of protecting her and Adeline is using her to torture me.

Lara slumps in her seat like sliding under the table, away from my gaze, is preferable to witnessing this exchange. In shielding her from Roy's shortcomings have I allowed her to create a myth around him—that if it weren't for me, he would have stuck around and been a good father. How can I compete with a fantasy?

I grab my father's mug and walk to the door. "I'll call you later, Lara."

I pause a beat hoping my daughter will stand up and join me. And when she doesn't, I force away the impulse to scoop her up, run her out of here, because she would hate me for treating her like a child. Some decisions are hers to make, even if it guts me to watch her make a mistake.

Adeline's eyes are the only set that meets mine, like a shove to the chest.

Roy and Lara sit fixed, looking at their empty plates, hungry for something that isn't on the menu. I push the door and reach back quickly, catching it before it slams.

With every step my legs tremble in protest, but I keep moving forward. I can't look back. Adeline might be perched at the window, cheering any evidence that she has inflicted pain. I blink over and over to clear my vision before pulling away.

The car accelerates and brakes, turns on dirt roads and goes straight for miles, uninterrupted, as if it is driving itself. And when I find myself in the Motel 6 parking lot, I am too stunned to get out of my car. I don't want to be here. I don't want to check-in. Worst of all, I don't want my daughter to stay at Adeline's and yet that's exactly where I've left her.

I think of my own parents, how pained they were when I chose to stay with Roy after he crashed the car following yet another drinking binge.

My mother cried, "You could have been with him. He could have killed you."

I flinch when I recall my flippant reply. "No, I would have been driving and there wouldn't have been an accident." There was no telling me, then. Just like I can't reason with my daughter, now.

As I drag myself out of the car, my phone vibrates in a string of quick, jerky buzzes, pent-up texts unloading from the queue.

mom
mom
where are u?
can u come back?
?
????
911

She's never used that before, but she knows the pact I made with her. *911. No questions asked. I'll come for you, day or night.*

I fire off a text and pull out, leaving a cloud of dust behind me as I hit the dirt road that brought me here.

■ ■ ■

Lara stands outside the mouth of the driveway, the overgrowth of twisted branches reach for her, like they want to pull her into their clutches. When she spots me, she pushes back her shoulders and blows out a breath.

I breathe in slowly as I pull over and remind myself *no running commentary or lectures, no pushing her into talking.* I sink my teeth into my lower lip to lock my mouth shut.

She barely waits for me to stop before she tugs at the handle and climbs in. Dropping her pocketbook between her knees she sighs and slams the door.

There is so much I want to say, to ask her; most of all, if she's all right.

"Sorry, honey. Bad reception."

She presses her face to the window, like she's getting one final look at the dreary landscape around her.

"I'll say!"

I wonder if she means my cell service or Adeline.

We drive for miles in silence. My head spins. What made her leave? But does it matter? She's with me now.

I grip the steering wheel tightly when she rubs the heel of her palm in her eye, her sniffles filling the space between us.

"Your father *does* love you." I don't add that the best he can give her might not be what she needs.

Lara's voice hiccups. "I know. But she's terrible, Mom. Terrible. I won't come here ever again. Dad will have to visit New York. It's the least he can do."

My wise, beautiful girl is smarter than I was when I was twice her age. I open my mouth, then close it. What is there for me to tell her that she hasn't already figured out?

So, I say nothing at all.

And neither does she, even when I drive past the motel and head onto the highway, back to the only home she's ever known. ■

WIND CHILL

Battling a wind sharp
from the northwest,
I trudge slowly around the stream-fed
small lake in the park, named
for a local environmentalist
who died before her time.
Hopeful signs posted here and there
picture likely wading birds
though none appear today.

The air stands at freezing
with wind chill,
but even in March there's no
ice or snow. I break off a stickery
handful of dry teasel for a bouquet
of sorts, and wonder when

the pond's marshy edges
will come alive with frog noise
and sun break through the mottled haze
that passes for sky—perhaps
when the accursed plague
lifts from the land. Then
the red-winged blackbird will
once more whisk from branch
to branch, whistling.

LYNN GILBERT

THEFT

As I drive northward, a storm
is rolling in from the west;
the sky is a deep sapphire
and the autumn trees
are trickling leaves
of every color but blue.

I'm smiling as if I owned
a safe-full of semi-precious stones:
garnet, malachite, topaz,
carnelian, jade, tiger's eye.
When the rain and strong winds
arrive here, the leaves
will come down in a hurry

and soon my jewelry box
will be burgled of every gem
but cardinal red
perched in deep emerald,
snow-laden firs.

LYNN GILBERT

CHALLENGER

DAN LEACH

August 1999

When I stepped into Miss Meechum's class for the first day of sixth grade, there were shoeboxes on all the desks and a message on the chalkboard that read: THE END OF THE WORLD IS ALMOST HERE. Having arrived early, I stood there, alone in that sunlit room smelling of old books and bleach, and I mumbled those words over and over, as if the incantation would surface the secret connection between doomsday and shoeboxes. I was twelve, an age where it is still possible to be moved by the mystery of endings.

When the rest of the kids showed up, everyone sat down at their desks, and Miss Meechum smiled her first-day-back smile. She asked about our summers. We told her we stayed home. Eventually, someone inquired about the shoeboxes, at which point Miss Meechum gestured towards the chalkboard and said, "Raise your hand if you've heard about Y2K."

My hand was among the raised, but secretly I was short on logistics. I knew Y2K had something to do with computers, something to do with banks, and possibly something to do with Jesus. Starting in the spring of that year, there was much talk about when the world was ending, but far less on why.

Like most twelve-year-olds, I had composed my existential stance in relation to my parents, who were divorced but still very much on speaking terms, especially where my education was concerned. I stayed with my mother, who was an emergency room nurse with the faith of a saint, and who spent the summer filling our garage with canned food, bottled water, and various other cataclysmic essentials. Dinner talk now included hypothetical apocalyptic scenarios. Night prayers danced around the possibility of a rapture. It wasn't that something would happen—it was that something *could* happen.

"I go by the preachers," my mother said. "The preachers say something's coming."

My father, a hospital administrator and noncommittal theist, mocked her for such views. He played an affable skeptic but offered little in the way of assurance. "We should be fine," was the closest he came to faith in the future, and I never liked the way his voice wavered on the word "should."

Now here was sweet Miss Meechum, on our first day back from summer, explaining to us that society was edging towards ruin, yet doing so with blue eyes that said, *Don't worry. Everything will be okay.* The ambiguity of the adult realm made you dizzy with fear but also wonder. It was unsettling but better (by far) than the tired normal.

"It's the zeros," Miss Meechum said. "Our computers could handle 1998, and they could handle 1999, but when 2000 comes, those zeros will cause everything to crash."

The word *crash* conjured images of skyscrapers imploding, their grey bases smashed to dust as if blasted by dynamite, their structures crumbling downwards to join the city-wide cloud of steel, glass, and concrete. I envisioned all the countries of all the continents, clear down to Antarctica, reduced simultaneously into fractured, worthless wastelands, all because some computers couldn't carry an extra zero. A whole world, hardly mine: crashed.

The picture evoked by Miss Meechum was more auspicious but not by much.

"What do you suppose will happen?" she asked, still blue-eyed and smiling. "When the power plants black out? When the airports no longer have radar? What about when the banks lose all their security?"

We thought about such questions and had no more insight than our parents. Then a girl in the front of the room raised her hand. She had pigtails the color of lemonade and braces that gave her words a wet, crackling quality. She was from California and had the posture of a natural genius long-bored with mediocrity.

"That's not going to happen," the girl said. "It's true there was a problem with the numbers, but they've fixed it. The transition into the new millennium will be fine."

"Where did you hear that?" asked Miss Meechum.

"My parents," said the girl. "But also the news."

Miss Meechum laughed as if a truly good joke had just been told. The girl from California glared.

"The news has one purpose," said Miss Meechum. "The sedation of the masses."

The girl's mouth let out a viciously moist click, a sound I took to mean, *This is nonsense. This is lunacy. I want to go back home to California.* Miss Meechum continued unfazed.

"Expect the best," she said. "But prepare for the worst. That's my philosophy."

Which brought us to the shoeboxes. Miss Meechum picked one up and held it out in front of her the way a parent might hold a swaddled infant.

"What is this?" she said, gently hefting the object.

"A shoebox," answered a brown-haired boy in the middle row.

"Wrong," said Miss Meechum. "This is a time capsule."

Something about that word in that moment stunned us, and we all looked at the boxes on our desks as if, because of Miss Meechum, they were no longer boxes at all. Mine was bright red with "NIKE" in white letters and, beneath that, the word "Challenger." I opened it up and peeked inside. It was clean and empty, and it smelled like tangerines. I loved it, immediately and deeply.

"From now until the new year," said Miss Meechum, "we're going to fill these with things that tell what it was like to be alive in Carolina at the end of the world. Items, pictures, writings. Your capsule will tell your story."

"Let me guess," said the girl from California. "After we fill them up, we're going to bury them." Miss Meechum nodded. The girl cackled.

"It would be tempting," Miss Meechum continued, "to view this as an act of preservation. But let me offer an alternative perspective. Instead of seeing this as a way to protect the past, think of it as a chance to communicate with the future."

"But if the world is ending," said the girl, "who will be here to find them?"

It was a strange look on Miss Meechum's face—not anger but not grace, not sadness but not joy, and nothing so readable as pity—when she looked down on the girl and said, "Maybe somebody. Maybe nobody. You tell me."

■ ■ ■

My father found the assignment morbid. My mother thought it was wonderful. They had been divorced since I was seven, and my father lived in a house across town, which made it easier to eavesdrop on their conversations, since the only way they could talk was over the phone.

I sat in the dark of my bedroom and listened, hoping for the same dumb thing I always hoped for when I eavesdropped— that finally some minor detail of my life would serve as the occasion for the two of them to remember how much they used to love each other, that my father would say "I'm sorry" for whatever it was that compelled him to leave, that my mother would say "You're forgiven" and "Come home," that I would reveal my presence with an explosion of laughter and ask the both of them "What the hell took you two so long?" Since their stated reason for separating was "We stopped making each other happy," and since I knew of no sin so egregious as to block the path back to our old life, I still hoped for reconciliation, even as I had learned to settle for cordiality.

"Kids have enough to worry about," my father said. "Why's a teacher adding death to the mix?"

"We're Christians," my mother said. "Death *is* the mix."

"*You* are a Christian," he said. "Junah's like me—a seeker. Plus, he's twelve. You know what I thought about when I was twelve? The Green Bay Packers, that's what. Vince Lombardi, Fuzzy Thurston. That and the Lone Ranger. Mind you, this was during Vietnam."

"Junah's not like you at all. He's a thinker."

"I'm not opposed to thinking," my father said. "But what's wrong with age-appropriate fixations?"

At this, my mother laughed her large-hearted, melodious laugh.

"What would those entail?" she said.

"I don't know," my father said. "Sports. Music. Girls."

Again I heard my mother's wonderful laughter, followed by my father's fairly average laughter, after which she whispered either "That sure sounds like fun" or "You don't know your son.

The next clear line belonged to my father, who said, "I know I'm old-fashioned, but the idea of a death box is creepy."

"Maybe Junah needs to be creeped out," my mother said. "I don't know about you, but I'm tired of everyone walking

I sat in the dark of my bedroom and listened, hoping for the same dumb thing I always hoped for when I eavesdropped...

around like 2000 is just another year. It's not. Something is about to happen."

A long silence followed this, one that said (on my father's end), "I can't talk about this anymore," and one that said (on my mother's end), "How could we talk about anything else?" They had been arguing about the millennium since spring and had arrived at the same impasse that marked so many of their other, smaller arguments, mainly, *There's no way to know who's right, so I guess we'll have to wait and see.*

Not long after this silence, they said goodnight and hung up. I got back in bed and fell asleep that night thinking about the assignment, and how it felt like I had been practicing my whole life to arrive here, at this one work of curation.

My mother had referred to me as a thinker, but that was misleading. More accurately, I was a rememberer and a nostalgia junky, a shy pariah from the South with a mind wired in reverse. Where most kids my age looked forward, I gazed back. Every piece of my past that should have faded— every face, every song, every leaf of every tree in the woods behind our house—it all got brighter in time. This made it difficult for me to think about the future. I always froze up when faced with questions about what I wanted for dinner, or what I planned to do on the coming weekend, or (worst of all) what I might become if the world did not end; yet, what peace I felt to lay back on my bed and roam the past for, say, the color of the scales on the mermaid that was tattooed on the forearm of the ex-Navy alcoholic who delivered mail to our home for several months in the fall of 1992. Deep turquoise with faint dabs of violet.

Finally, thanks to the assignment, I could treat the future as I had always understood it—a singular event for the recovery of the past.

■ ■ ■

Miss Meechum said our capsules needed to tell a story. I did not have one of those, not yet at least, so I decided to start with photographs.

First photograph: my family (before the divorce). Here are the three of us standing in front of our house on Christmas morning. We have come out onto the lawn in our pajamas— my father, my mother, and me—to watch the first fakes of snow drifting down from the sky. My parents are looking at me, and I am looking up, and everyone is smiling, there in the yard, by the Japanese maple whose wine-red leaves are jeweled with snow. If you are wondering why we look surprised, it's because it almost never snows in Carolina. If you are wondering why we look as happy as we have ever been, it's because we are. Take note, survivor: these are my people.

Second photograph: The Pipe. I thought about giving you a picture of my room, but since I spent more time in The Pipe than in my room, and since (according to Miss Meechum) the goal here was for you to understand something about me, this seemed like the better contribution. As you can see, The Pipe was an old drainage tube in the woods behind our house. It had not drained anything for as long as we had lived there, since the creeks at either end were dried up, but it appeared at the base of a leafy hill like the entrance to some forgotten cave. You could enter The Pipe at one end and, with a slight stoop, walk the fifty feet of concrete tunnel (the middle of which was cool and dark) then emerge back into the light on the other side of the hill. When I was younger, it accommodated fantasy. It was the dungeon where the princess was trapped. It was the haunted caverns where the pirate king hid his treasure. As I got older, it became a place to hide. Sometimes I was hiding from the heat of a summer day. Sometimes I was hiding from the world. If there is anything to be gleaned from a person's preferred geography, hold this one close.

Third photograph: my bookshelf. If the libraries of the new world are lost beneath the rubble, and if a search-and-rescue team is assembled to descend into the wreckage to retrieve a small cache of titles, consider this photograph a modest kind of manifest. Start with the Tolkien, all of the Tolkien, then move on to *Earthsea* and *Watership Down*. *Hatchet* is essential, as is *The Outsiders*. From the shelf in the middle with the comics, take *Watchmen, Bone*, and Miller's *Dark Knight*. For classics, you cannot go wrong with Flannery, and Faulkner is fun if you like feeling drunk in the middle of a paragraph. I didn't have siblings or friends. Books had to (and did) suffice. There are better shelves out there, I am sure, but this one is mine.

■ ■ ■

The next day, Miss Meechum had us write a letter of introduction to place in the time capsule. Mine was brief, including only my name (Junah, after my father), my age (twelve), and the reason for my composing the capsule (which was not only to appease Miss Meechum, but also to see what there was to say about the place I was in and the people all around me). I finished the letter in three sentences, neatly folded the paper into a snug triangle, and placed it in the capsule alongside the photographs and the plastic dashboard Jesus I stole from my mother's van.

Three sentences felt sufficient, especially for an introduction, but when Miss Meechum read it, she said it was "criminally concise" and "wildly impersonal."

"All logistics," she said. "No heart."

"Does this mean I have to write a new letter?"

"Yes," she said. "This time leave some blood on the page. Give me one paragraph on your deep wounds and another paragraph on your deep loves. Due tomorrow, no excuses."

After school that day, I went to The Pipe. No one was there, and it was quiet, and the way the light fell at both ends made it feel natural to lay one word in front of the next. I wrote, beginning with my deep wounds. How I was shorter than everyone else (much shorter), and how my size brought on many years of verbal and physical abuse. I wrote about how I suffered from a speech impediment (a bad one), and how this handicap caused me to hate myself and doubt my language. I wrote about how lonely it feels to grow up in the South as an only child with a body that wouldn't grow and a voice that doesn't work, and how sometimes this particular constellation of weirdness made me want to kill myself. The paragraph ran for three pages (front and back). I had no idea my wounds were so generative.

The paragraph on my deep loves was even longer, as it included all the books I loved, and all the songs I loved, and all the things I loved about living where I did, which were too many things to count. I wrote about my mother, an emergency room nurse who caught fire for Christ when I was two. I wrote about my father, a hospital admin with a deep need for Clemson football. The Saturdays we used to dress up in orange and drive down to Death Valley, and the Sundays we used to wake up early to worship at the Methodist church down the road. I told about their divorce, and about my continued hope in their coming back together. I told about The Pipe, and about the half-acre yard with the Japanese maple out front, and about the pool down the street we used to walk to in the summer.

The next day, I showed the new pages to Miss Meechum, and she said, "Finally, some blood."

■ ■ ■

After Miss Meechum's class was Coach Mac, who taught History. Coach Mac's first words: "You are not a child anymore, so don't act like one!"

The proximate apparatus supported Coach Mac's thesis. Behind the school, instead of a sandbox and a playground, there was a football field and a track. In the hallways, instead of brightly colored murals and cubby boxes, there were grey walls and steel lockers. The desks you sat in, the books they gave you, even the food they served for lunch—all of it was heavier, with sharper edges. All of it was screaming, *You are here to become an adult!*

It was a strange thing to be told, in one breath, that the world was ending, and in the next breath, that you needed to grow up just in time to die. If middle school taught me anything, it was this: make peace with contradiction.

■ ■ ■

Among the students at my school, nothing was less cool than admitting you loved the world enough to feel blue over its ending. You could be grizzled and apocalyptic, such as Sarah Winters, who said, "It's about damn time someone put a stop to this shitshow," or you could be tranquil and indifferent, such as Matt Sumpter, who said, "We had a good run, but nothing lasts forever." What you couldn't be was enamored, and since no one was more enamored than me, no one was less cool than me. I was mocked but not sorry. All these lovely people walking around with their weird secrets and untold stories—not only did I not want the world to end, I wanted it to last forever.

■ ■ ■

Me: "Hey, Dad, do you think it's dumb to love the world?"
Him: "Absolutely."
Me: "Why? Because it's ugly and full of death?"
Him: "No. Because no matter how well you love it, the world will always break your heart."
Me: "What then? Become a cynic? I'm only twelve."
Him: "Hell no. Cynicism is cowardly. Better dumb and broken-hearted than spineless and clever."
Me: "You're not leaving me a lot of options here. Either way I come out grifted."
Him: "Welcome to living."

■ ■ ■

After several weeks of adding items to the time capsule, it occurred to me that ours is a project of trust. You are trusting me to include only the most significant objects, objects which, once arranged, will tell you a story. I am trusting you to receive these objects and form certain connections. We are, the both of us, divorced by time and bound up in contingencies.

■ ■ ■

Take the plastic dashboard Jesus that I stole from my mother's van. If you favor sincerity, you might find this relic and intuit that it symbolizes my religious convictions. If, on the other hand, your interpretations tend towards cynicism, you might see this figurine as some kind of critique of commodified spirituality.

Both readings would be wrong. I included the plastic Jesus because of my mother. Before my father left, my mother was casual in her faith. After he left, she became something of a fanatic, though not for institutional religion so much as the person of Jesus Christ. My mother loved Christ so much she viewed believers as His beloved bride, and the world as a temporary situation. "A vapor," she often called it. "A prelude."

She would quote the Apostle Peter, who said believers are "strangers and pilgrims" in this world. She would quote the Apostle Paul, who said believers are "citizens of heaven." This was not mere theology. This was her life and her faith and her hope, and if the world was going to end, she intended to see her only child saved before it did.

I wanted to believe, but I could not shake the questions. First and foremost: the scandal of invisibility.

"If Christ loves us," I asked her one night. "Wouldn't He want us to see Him?"

"He does let us see Him," she said. "In The Bible. In Christ."

"That's not the same. I want to see Him like I see you. I want to talk to Him like we're talking now."

There was a look that came over my mother's face whenever I expressed such doubts. It wasn't a look of disappointment or frustration. In fact, it was almost a look of sympathy, as if she felt sorry that I lacked the imagination to envision a Christ who was ever-present yet never-visible, ever-speaking yet never-audible. It was the look you would

This was her life and her faith and her hope, and if the world was going to end, she intended to see her only child saved before it did.

give to a child who is trying his best to solve a math problem, except that, no matter how many times he adds it up, he can never arrive at the correct sum.

"He is out there," she said. "Just because you cannot see Him, it doesn't mean He isn't out there."

"Where is Out There?"

There was a window by my bed. She tapped her fingernail against the glass. "Heaven," she said. When she was gone, I lay on my bed and stared up at the sky, which was no longer the sky because now it was a window between Jesus's house and mine.

"Christ?" I asked the window. "You home?"

From the window came nothing. Just an abundance of blackness and a few stars and, poking like a baby's head over the tops of the trees, the rounded dome of the moon.

I remembered my mother's fingernail tapping against the glass. I got dressed and went outside. I gathered all the rocks I could find and began throwing them at the sky. I wanted to see His face in the window. Failing that, I wanted to put a crack in the divide between Out There and In Here. Like my father said—more seeker than believer.

How much of this story will you excavate from a plastic figurine? And if the answer is "None," what will you tell in its place?

The longer this thing continues, the more it occurs to me: this is your story, not mine. I pack and bury the box, but the resurrection is on you.

■ ■ ■

The assignment requires me to tell you about my place, and I love my place, yet I am weary of pickled riffing about the South. Oh the mountains! Oh the beaches! Oh the green sprawling cities that make the wide streets of Elsewhere seem lovely as used floss! This is all true, but I am tired of the truth and all its sprawling implications.

My father once told me that you could learn more about a man from the contents of his pockets than from any story he told you about himself. This, then, is how I will tell you about the place that I love, which is the South. I will empty the pockets of this strange and wonderful place. You arrange.

■ ■ ■

Pocket artifact number one: the other night, right as I was falling asleep, I heard the sound of someone knocking on our door. I answered it, and it was the boy from across the street.

"Follow me!" he said. "I have something to show you!"

I didn't tell my mother I was leaving. I just slipped out and followed this boy to a cul-de-sac, where a street-lamp had carved a circle of light onto the rain-slick pavement. In that circle was a lump, grey and still, no bigger than a fist.

"It's a bat," whispered the kid. "And he's dead."

This last fact gave me confidence. I drew closer. The little bones in its wings, his silent pink face: I stared deeply at the place where his eyes should have been. I felt that this was all wrong, and I wanted to bury him.

"Don't touch him," the kid said. "He's dead."

I heard this but bent down anyway and lifted him by his wing into the light. For a moment the wing was a backlit map with veins that ran wild with rivers. There were many odd-shaped countries carved out in tiny bones.

I held him and knew what needed to happen.

"I have to bury him," I said to the kid.

I was going to say more, but before I could, the bat came alive in my hand. There was the flapping, then the screeching, then the angry mouth swinging around to sink its teeth into my thumb. I released him, but he refused to release me.

After it was over and the bat had flown of, we just stood there in the cul-de-sac and stared at the blood that was leaking out of my hand. I was laughing. The kid was crying. Neither of us could have said why.

Later that night, I woke up from a deep sleep, and my hand was on fire with pain. Because of the darkness of my room, and because of how intense the pain was, I thought the bat had returned and was biting me again. I turned on the lights to calm myself down. I had to say, out loud and more than once, "You are alone here. He is out there." I had to remind myself that I had been let go.

■ ■ ■

Miss Meechum said that the starting point of any composition is listening, in which I was well-practiced. Consider this interaction, which happens (if I'm lucky) about three times a week.

"You're kind of quiet," some kid says to me.

I nod my head, so as to imply *Correct.*

"Why's that?" they ask.

"Speech impediment."

They scrunch their faces, so as to imply *What the hell did you just say?*

I repeat myself, slower, as practiced: "Speech impediment."

Cue the Southern sense of sympathy: "That sucks, man. I'm sorry."

"Don't be," I say. "It means I get to listen."

■ ■ ■

What do you make of this picture of me? Apparently, I have a look on my face (natural, not affected) that communicates confusion. My mother describes it as "stunned." My father's word is "lost." One classmate said, "You look like you just woke up from a dream, except you're mad at us for having brought you out of it."

■ ■ ■

Miss Meechum told us to contribute an item that a survivor might find helpful. I thought about leaving you my Swiss Army knife, but instead I went with my sunglasses. One day, when I was five, and when my father still lived with us, I was rummaging around in his garage and found these, all massive and black, the kind which certain elderly folks wear to block out the sun and all of humanity. They were heavy on my face, and I loved the heaviness. I loved having that big, thick piece of dark between myself and the world. I put them on and, for the next few years, I did not take them off. I wear them, even in The Pipe, even after dark.

Take Career Day at Northwood Middle. Career Day meant much talk from parents who were bankers, contractors, and shop owners. It also meant free floss from the dentist and going outside to climb into the cab of a firetruck. The firemen were large, bearded men who let us play with the sirens, and who gave us red plastic helmets.

When the presentations were over, Coach Mac walked to the chalkboard and wrote, "In 100 words or more, describe your dream job."

I chewed on the end of my pencil, pretending to think about it, but I already knew what my dream job was. I wanted a job where I was left alone all day with absolutely nothing to do. Since no one would bother me, and since I had nothing to do, I would spend my work days reading books and writing stories and taking long naps in which I dreamed about things I had read in the books and written in the stories. I would never miss a day of work for a job such as this.

I once made the mistake of sharing this dream with my parents. They said reading and writing were "attractive skills" and suggested jobs like college professor and copy editor, both of which were laughable compromises.

For the purposes of Coach Mac's writing prompt, I got creative. I wrote: "My dream job is to be the toll taker on a road that dead ends in a ghost town."

Coach held me after class to discuss this response.

"Let's talk about being a toll taker," he said. "What specifically interests you about this job?" I explained to him that I would only consider positions at toll stations on roads that people no longer used—ghost towns, abandoned highways, half-built bridges, et cetera.

"I don't understand," he said. "What would be the point of being a toll taker if there were no drivers to pass your station?"

"The point would be to get your time back."

"Are you saying that jobs steal your time?"

"Yes."

"Do you think that school steals your time?"

"Yes."

"You want a job where you will do nothing. Is that right?"

"No," I said. "I want a job where I don't have to do anything. That way, I can do what I want to do."

"Which is?"

"Remembering, more than anything. But also reading and some napping, too."

Coach Mac looked disturbed by this. I asked him if he was going to call my home. He said that unless I could think of another response, he felt it was his duty to contact my parents.

"Firefighter," I said. "I could also be a firefighter."

Coach handed me a fresh sheet of paper and requested I write a new paragraph. He left me alone, and I was happy to oblige.

■ ■ ■

Early one Saturday morning, my mother caught me in The Pipe as I was deciding which of my many gemstones I would put inside the capsule. I had it down between my two favorites: a bright amethyst the size of a small egg, or a smooth little heart-shaped jasper shot through with forest greens and chocolate browns.

"Hey," my mother said. "You're spending a lot of time with that box. It feels like you're making it into something more."

"What exactly is your concern?"

"I know how you are," she said. "And I don't want you to lose yourself in making this thing, okay?"

I said, "Yes, ma'am," and my mother left me alone, at which point, I emptied the contents of my capsule onto the cool pavement of The Pipe and began, as I had so many times before, arranging and rearranging all of the items, in order to see how each new arrangement unearthed a different story. I would do this work all day. I would do this work until it got dark, at which point I would go home, eat dinner, and lay in my bed so as to happily do the same work all over again: break, build, arrange, repeat.

My mother had said, "I know how you are." She was not wrong. There is nothing I would rather have done than lose every last ounce of myself in the act of composition.

■ ■ ■

I loved the world, but the world often horrified me, especially the eyes. We did not yet have words like 'social anxiety' or 'introverted personality.' All I knew was that wherever I was—the classroom, or the cafeteria, or some scrubby little field built to host a barely enjoyable sport—all proximate eyes seemed aimed, for reasons I couldn't fathom, at me. I hated those eyes. I preferred home. I preferred to be alone and, if possible, reading. Sunglasses saved me. With those on, I was still the watched but also the watcher.

■ ■ ■

Everyone at Northwood Middle had decided that, since the world was ending, you had better fall in love before it did. Except they refused to call it falling in love. They called it getting "bit."

"I saw you holding hands with Brooke. You bit?"

"Yeah, man. I'm bit."

Based on what I heard, I gathered that preemptive confession was ideal.

"You guys know that new girl from Georgia?"

"Yeah."

"She bit me."

"No way."

"Yeah, man. She bit me hard."

I was unaware that this terminology was regional until I attended a family reunion, where an out-of-state cousin asked about a friend who had accompanied me.

"Ryan seems like a great guy," she said. "Is he dating anyone?"

"Ryan's all used up," I said. "He has nothing left."

"Why's that?"

"He got bit by a girl from Charleston who left him for some drummer."

"Bit?" she said. "What are you talking about?"

She was from Waco, Texas and looked at me like I was from another planet.

■ ■ ■

I would not have minded falling in love before the end of the world, but first there was this business of getting saved. I wanted to talk to Christ about all that getting saved entailed, but Christ was Out There, and I was not. I was In Here, with the assignment and the questions and the sense that, if there was something like salvation to be found, it was waiting for you to come to it. The question was not, "Could you find it?" The question was, "Would you want to?" A mind is a hard thing to leave behind.

■ ■ ■

Christ was Out There, but even with the world ending, He refused to show His face. My curiosity demanded an appearance; eventually, I settled for a clue. The clue came during a Sunday morning service that was so boring, I had no choice but to remove the Bible from the pew in front of me and begin reading.

I held the Bible by its spine and let the pages fall where they may. Split open before me was chapter fourteen of John's Gospel. To double down on the sense of destiny, I resisted the urge to begin reading at the top of the left page. I closed my eyes, brought the book to my face, and resolved to read whatever verse was directly in view.

And what I saw was this: "If anyone loves Me, he will keep My word; and My Father will love him, and We will come to him and make our home with him."

If this verse was true, I had reversed the operation through which it became possible to know Christ. I had been searching

I knew this was not the answer my mother wanted, but it was honest, and it was necessary. I was not ready to believe in ghosts. I was barely cutting it as a seeker.

for Christ Out There, throwing my rocks and demanding to see His face, when here in the plain words of the Nazarene, the exact opposite was laid out—Him making a home In Here. All this time I had been waiting for an invitation, when apparently He was waiting for the same thing.

I asked my mother that night, "Is it true that, if you ask Him, Christ will make His home inside your heart?"

"Yes," she said. "He comes in as The Holy Ghost."

"What does it feel like?"

My mother thought about this for a long time. Then she said, "Have you ever lost something, and it stays lost for a long time, but then you find it and feel very grateful?"

"Sure."

"That's what The Holy Ghost feels like. Familiar but also new. In John chapter three, Jesus compares Him to the wind."

"Why the wind?"

"Because you can't see Him, but you can feel Him. Because His movements are wholly beyond your control. And because there is nowhere on Earth that He is not."

We sat there for a while, neither of us saying anything.

"I can pray with you," she eventually said. "I can ask The Holy Ghost to come into your heart. Would you like that?"

"Not right now," I said. "But maybe later."

I knew this was not the answer my mother wanted, but it was honest, and it was necessary. I was not ready to believe in ghosts. I was barely cutting it as a seeker.

■ ■ ■

"Tell the future something about violence," Miss Meechum said. "Then tell it something about love." To understand the violence back here, there is one name you should know: Rusty Riggins.

Rusty Riggins liked to sneak up behind you, lock a sleeper hold around your neck, and lift you several inches of the ground so that everyone could see your legs spasm as you tried not to black out. You always blacked out, and, once you did, Rusty would drop you on the ground, steal whatever was in your pockets, and culminate his assault by one final abuse, such as drawing cartoon genitalia on your face in permanent marker, or throwing one of your shoes into the upper branches of a pine.

Rusty had never bullied me, but I didn't mistake this for fortuity. He simply needed more time. I knew this because his victims and I shared certain qualities, mainly being small, quiet, and alone.

For love: Sadie Hayes. I had only shared this love one time and with one person, who was my mother. I told her that I was bit, and she asked who, and I told her Sadie, and the look of disgust on her face was not a fun thing to suffer.

"Sadie Hayes?" she said. "The Scab-eater?"

Calling Sadie a scab-eater was not, technically speaking, mean-spirited. In fact, my mother could not have offered a more objective observation. At school, Sadie had been seen picking, studying, and consuming her own scabs so habitually, so plainly, so unapologetically, everyone called her Sadie the Scab-eater. I had never actually spoken to Sadie, but I had heard that, when Miss Meechum explained to her that eating scabs was "inappropriate," and that some of the other students had complained, Sadie looked Miss Meechum dead in the eye and said, "I don't care what other people find appropriate."

It wasn't just the scab thing. Sadie's insularity was holistic. Back in elementary school, she had wild auburn hair that she refused to brush. Instead, she wrapped the whole tangled mess of it into some kind of lopsided nest that sat on top of her head with the help of camouflage head-wrap. Back then, which is when I first fell for her, her clothes were mismatched, over-sized, sometimes-dirty, and often inside-out. At recess, when other students played, Sadie read books; and in class, when other students participated, Sadie slept. Between the scab eating and the apathy, everyone thought she was gross. But they were wrong. Sadie was original. She was, as far as I could tell, the one person who was inoculated to the virus that plagued everyone else—the need to be loved.

The summer between fifth and sixth grade, Sadie went full punk, and this moved me. She shaved both sides of her head, leaving a thin strip on top, which she dyed neon green and twisted into spikes using Elmer's Glue. She pierced her lip, both eyebrows, and her septum, all in one night, and all using only a safety pin and a bottle of hydrogen peroxide. For clothing, if Sadie wore it, it was black. The leather bomber jacket and the combat boots from the Army-Navy Surplus. The chokers and the studded cuffs. The revolving door of ratty shirts for bands like Bad Brains, Rancid, and The Dead Kennedys.

I was made uncomfortable by my mother's reaction, but I was not ashamed.

"That's right," I said. "Sadie the Scab-eater."

"There are plenty of other—"

"It's Sadie."

My mother shook her head and changed the subject. For a long time to come, we left the subject changed.

■ ■ ■

I called my father and asked him about Sadie.

Me: "You think it's weird to fall for a girl who eats scabs?"

Him: "I once fell for a girl who ate pig's feet. It didn't last, but that's no fault of the pigs."

Me: "What's your point? Different strokes for different folks?"

Him: "Not exactly. More like, love's too high a thrill for nitpickers."

Me: "I like that."

Him: "You should. It's the truth."

■ ■ ■

I did not ask Sadie Hayes to be my girlfriend for the same reason I did not ask The Holy Ghost into my heart. Because everything was safe when viewed at a distance. But to close that distance, to get close, to get so close that someone could take of your sunglasses and stare into your soul—nothing was more horrifying than that.

■ ■ ■

Maybe this is why I feel so close to you: because of this distance between us that will never be closed.

■ ■ ■

Miss Meechum told us to copy out our three favorite quotations and put them in the time capsule. In went Thomas Wolfe, who said, "The whole conviction of my life now rests upon the belief that loneliness, far from being a rare and curious phenomenon, peculiar to myself and to a few other solitary men, is the central and inevitable fact of human existence."

In went Howlin' Wolf, who said, "There ain't nothing but my troubles."

In went my father, who said, "Take heart. For people living on loaned breaths, it's really not that bad."

■ ■ ■

The Holy Ghost wanted detonation rights to my heart, but so did all the other little bombs. I attended the third best public middle school in Taylors, South Carolina, where stories buried themselves like mines in your brain and left you, after you'd heard them, waiting for the inevitable explosion.

Some older boy at the lunch table would start it: "There's a perv in Del Norte who hands out tampered candy every

Halloween. Razor blades in Reese Cups. Anthrax in Pixie Sticks."

You had about seven seconds to contemplate this before someone else started in: "My cousin knows a guy who tapes infected needles to gas pump handles. By the time you realize what stuck you, it's too late."

Each new bomb would be more vile than the last, until someone said something that was too horrible to follow.

"My dad told me about this place he went to in college. It was called a glory hole. You could slip your dick through a hole in the wall and, on the other side, there'd be a whore who would suck you of. Except this one night, instead of a whore on the other side, there was a psychopath with a pair of garden shears."

You left these conversations and returned to a classroom where Miss Meechum would read aloud a passage from Twain, expecting it to thrill you. The sentences were nice, and you saw where someone might come away with a new perspective, but after the bombs of the cafeteria, literature hit with the force of a nursery rhyme. You sensed on such days that you had arrived at a place beyond the reach of language, possibly beyond the reach of love and of Christ, a place where only more filth (and possibly good music) could remind you how it felt to be alive.

■ ■ ■

I thought about telling Sadie Hayes that I loved her. I tried to use the end of the world as a catalyst for confidence. It worked until I saw her, at which point my already-broken voice became a pure failure. I continued to pray. Courage, too, detonates on its own terms.

■ ■ ■

"Draw close to Him," said my mother, the other night, after prayers. "And He will draw close to you." "Closeness freaks me out."

"Give me your hand," she said. "I want to pray for you."

I gave her my hand and half-listened to her sweet words. But while she prayed, my mind reeled backwards, stunned by the bomb about the glory hole and the garden shears.

"How about now?" she said. "Will you make space in your heart?"

"Not yet," I told her. "My heart's a bit cluttered right now."

■ ■ ■

By the end of August, my capsule was cluttered. The rocks and the letters and the photographs; the pages torn from comic books and the tools stolen from my father's workbench; a Swiss Army knife and a map to the Appalachian Trail. The leaves outside the window were wine-red and fewer by the day. The talk about the end of the world was ongoing and increasingly serious. I carried a love that I could not speak and a fear that I could not name. My mother continued stockpiling. My father told me everything was going to be okay. I did not know what else to do, so I kept filling up the capsule. I told myself that when you read this—if you ever read this—you would know what needs to be done. ■

GODPAINED

I spoke to God so much as a child that
when he vanished—when I dissolved
him—he left a hole in my head. An
aperture my brain   developed around.
I still talk into it sometimes. I still hold
people up and see if they fit.

HAYLEY PHILLIPS

SÉANCE

A lake, contained, containing.
When I deplete my lungs the
water takes me easier because
I put myself at its mercy, no
reserves, no contingencies—it
gives me things. Because I let
it hold my life for a minute
without cheating—I've earned
something at the bottom
where water meets earth
and people hide their gods.
I want an answer, to graze my
toes along whatever gelatinous
gut-dropping thing is down there
and ask you stupid questions like
why.

HAYLEY PHILLIPS

ERIN
KEANE

t a greasy spoon in Louisville, Erin Keane dissects a phrase she holds in particular contempt: *It was a different time.* She spits it out over the clatter of dishes and shouted orders coming from the nearby kitchen, rolling her expressive eyes for good measure. The weaselly wording, she believes, offers a "get-out-of-problematic-jail-free card" to people and to our culture-at-large in the face of the #MeToo movement.

She moves easily between contemporary examples and the notorious case—and subsequent cancellation—of recently deceased Jerry Lee Lewis, who married his thirteen-year-old cousin Myra Gail Brown in 1957 when he was twenty-two. Already, Keane points out, Lewis's obituary is being smoothed over, just as it was when "hottie Dennis Quaid" and "Winona Ryder, the coolest girl in the world" starred in the airbrushed 1989 biopic *Great Balls of Fire.* "At what point in time are we not living in a different time?" she asks. "We're always living in someone's past."

This observation, and the need for a deeper, serious reckoning with our treatment of young girls and women, is at the heart of Keane's debut nonfiction book *Runaway: Notes on the Myths that Made Me.* As editor in chief of *Salon* and an influential culture writer in her own right, Keane has crafted her own brand of incisive, pithy commentary on topics including film and television, the intersection of cocktails and self-care—her Fascinator is particularly good—the wholesome sex appeal of Kentucky's Democratic governor and, more recently, a passionate ode to and defense of Standard Time. So it makes sense that *Runaway*, a linked essay collection, combines cultural criticism and intrepid journalism with the complicated history of Keane's own family.

In resonant, probing prose, she recounts how her mother left her Kansas home at thirteen in 1970 to spend the next few years as a runaway, hitchhiking across the country, living on the road and in communes. Two years later, when she was only fifteen but claimed to be in her twenties, she met and married Keane's father, who was thirty-six.

Keane's father died when Keane was five, and the stories that sprang up in the wake of his death hovered over her childhood and adolescence. While *Runaway* untangles many of those myths, Keane's observant eye, trained from years as a

Erin Keane   *photo by Alix Mattingly*

poet, focuses on her mother, a dynamic character who refuses to classify herself as a victim. What results is an interrogation of how Keane herself looks at her family and the world. She writes, "I keep circling back to the stories that should have been told about girls and women but were instead given over to men, and my own complicity in perpetuating these narrative imbalances and injustices."

After receiving praise from the *Los Angeles Times* ("a deeply felt family memoir that also functions as an exegesis of our social texts") and other publications, *Runaway* was named one of NPR's Best Books of 2022.

As her grilled cheese and fries grew increasingly cold, Keane—a previous contributor to *Appalachian Review*—spoke with the magazine's editor Jason Kyle Howard about the creative and emotional journey she followed in writing *Runaway*, how things have changed—or not—for young girls in our culture and how the book might contribute to our current conversation about the #MeToo movement.

■ ■ ■

JASON KYLE HOWARD: The book opens with your focus on [Woody Allen's 1978 movie] *Manhattan* and deconstructing that film. Could you talk about the impetus for that? When [did] you [know] this would become a book?

ERIN KEANE: 2015 was when I sort of wrote the very first… little short commentary reflecting on *Manhattan* in light of Mariel Hemingway's memoir [*Out Came the Sun*] and the anecdote that she tells…about Woody Allen afterwards [how he attempted to seduce her as a teenager].

And going back to that movie—I think there's sometimes a tendency, especially online, when we're writing these sort of quick, cultural-pegged commentaries to kind of come in with the argument angle, with the opinion, the commentary on it, from a point of view of *Well, any right-thinking person would know that this was problematic, and I have always known that, like I was born knowing that this is wrong.* It comes from [the feeling that] you have to argue kind of forcefully to cut through the noise online, and you have to make your points really fast because people don't give you a lot of time.

But from that I think we lose the space to talk about how we learn and how we evolve. And I think when we lose the space to talk about that we also potentially lose bringing readers along who might not have already arrived at that same conclusion of *This is a problem and I'm going to tell you why.* They might still be over here going like, *Wait a second, I thought we all knew these were good movies, that's what I've always been told.*

So I just sort of felt like I couldn't *not* hold myself accountable [because] I was somebody who loved this movie and cited it and quoted from it and used it as a frame of reference for a lot of other cultural writing that I had done, and I had moved away from that because I just simply lost a taste for his work in light of [his daughter Dylan Farrow's] allegations [of sexual abuse] being sort of resurfaced. And I was able to read them as an adult and hear her adult voice [now and] not the sort of *way-back time to the '90s* when all of that stuff was playing out for the first time.

JKH: Do you think that that approach reaches a different segment or has the potential to reach a different segment of readers? I'm so taken with that opening and how you constructed it, and your honesty, accountability, and

vulnerability. You're functioning almost as a stand-in for people in the culture who might've been on the fence or in this moment of *Well, yeah, I've heard this, but let's go see the film.*

EK: Right. There are a lot of ways that you could have dismissed the notion that maybe these films are not as harmless as they had been positioned to be: *Well this is art over here, and then there's gossip over here,* or *There's the art and the artist, and we don't have to confuse them.* And in reading deeper about [this]— especially from women critics [writing] contemporaneously during the 90s when… [Allen] basically managed to avoid things falling apart for him personally and professionally but really only through what I've come to understand is an enormous amount of privilege and an enormous amount of power that is exerted on the press and on public opinion.

But am I trying to function as a stand-in? I don't know about that but I do feel that it wasn't going to serve anybody for me to come in being like so, *Woody Allen movies are trash and everyone knows that.* Because I wanted to leave space for people to come in and say like *Look, I was also very taken,* and also it's just a way to avoid being called out for being a hypocrite too—like, *This you?* 'Cause I can't avoid the writing I've done, this wasn't just—

JKH: *[Here are the] receipts!*

EK: Exactly. There's no way to avoid it so you might as well just state the embarrassing truth yourself which is something we do in nonfiction writing. When we're writing truthfully about ourselves, we make ourselves vulnerable in order to gain the trust of the reader also.

JKH: And to be invitational…

EK: Because I think also there is sometimes the tendency—and these are the dismissive tendencies, right? *It was a different time.* And people love to say that because it absolves literally everyone from accountability. But we know—students of history know, people who have just been alive a little while in the world know—that even during that quote-unquote *different time* there have always been the dissenting voices who have pointed out when things are actually morally wrong, to use a sort of word that I feel like I probably would've chafed against in the 90s because it would've felt like a morality that was telling me that I was wrong.

But…some things just violate the bonds of humanity and throughout history there have always been people to sort of say that. And that's something that I tried to do in the book overall was to show, to really dismantle the idea of *It was a different time.*

I feel like that's something that lets the people involved in the past story off the hook, but it also I think functions as this sort of get-out-of-problematic-jail free card for all of us, because at what point in time are we *not* living in a different time? We're always living in someone's past. So I think instead we can say *there was a different dominant culture at work.* Maybe there was a different cultural agreement because the cultural gatekeepers were cisgender straight white men—Christian men for the most part, but not exclusively—and they dictated what was considered acceptable by them and therefore what people who wanted to get along within the systems that they perpetuated had to then go agree with.

People don't want to have to reckon with how the power imbalance has always benefitted men over girls, because a lot of times it is your own—like in mine—it's your own family.

It's easier to say *Well it was a different time, it was more accepted that my grandma was married off at fourteen to a nineteen-year-old, twenty-year-old boy.* And it's like... why do you think it was okay then but it's not okay now? Is there something that's changed fundamentally about fourteen-year-old girls in the last seventy years? Not enough.

JKH: No. Not enough. When did you know that you were going to write about your parents' relationship? Obviously, the book focuses on your mother as a runaway. But...I'm suspecting that there might have been a lot of focus in the beginning on your father, and on interpreting his story, discovering his story and then shifting to focus maybe [on your mother].

EK: Well, [the shift came] in the reporting. So I wrote that first essay in 2015—so [this is a] roundabout way back to your question of how did this become a book—and then...I put it out there and I actually didn't show my mother that story...I sort of made an impulsive decision to lay the family out there a little bit without asking. And I didn't feel like I did too much, but it was just enough that I was like *maybe we'll just let that one simmer on the back burner a little bit—*

JKH: And see what happens, and how it plays.

EK: Yeah. And you know, it had a little bit of virality at the time. It got a lot of good mentions [online] and then it kind of went away again. And then [the] fall of 2017 the Harvey Weinstein exposé came out. So we had already been working in this mode of like there's Bill Cosby, there's a couple of others, Woody Allen, also, a couple of other sort of high-profile men who had had these allegations against them that had been long-standing... but I think [were] finally being taken a little more seriously. And I do sort of in a lot of ways attribute that to millennials coming of age and being out there in the media and in the workforce, being adults and reflecting back on their childhood now.

JKH: That's right.

"A moving, razor-sharp memoir."
—D. Watkins, *New York Times* best-selling author of *The Beast Side*

Runaway

Notes on the Myths that Made Me

ERIN KEANE

EK: I'm the young end of Gen X, and we are just simply not a very big generation. We had a much harder time affecting cultural sea change. But millennials could match the Boomers, you know? Because they made them. So that suddenly was like oh wait, even if there's no conviction, it's no longer gossip over here, it's actually—this is news, we can corroborate, we can substantiate, we can actually build reporting out of this that can be serious and have repercussions, cultural and in some cases legal repercussions.

So when that happened I actually then started, for the first time in my life, thinking about my family's story also in light of #MeToo. And I started this project with the intention of writing a book to try to understand how my father could have made this choice because he died when I was five. So I can't ask him, it's unknowable. And so I think that the unknowable and the mystery is always more attractive to me as a writer with a journalism background because I have a lot of questions. That's where I thought all the questions [lay].

JKH: I always think about how absence is presence, you know, in a big way—

EK: He was this mythical creature in my life and in my own personal mythology, and it was this major loss that was a foundational thing to me. It was a foundational part of my identity as a writer—as somebody who wrote about loss, wrote about never remembering a time in my life when loss wasn't a major presence in it. So I thought, *I'll start with an essay for Father's Day.* Of course it was a Father's Day essay, right? [laughs] So I called my mother and I said, "Hey, can I interview you for this? I have questions that I don't know the answers to."

My mother is a great storyteller and has a repertoire of stories that she would tell about her younger life. I knew she had been a runaway...I knew that she went by Alexis, because we still have family and friends who call her Alexis from the old days. It was very normal to me to have a mother who was known by different identities to different people. But I wanted to know things like *Tell me about your first date. Tell me about the first time you met.* I wanted to say there's a point you could go back to in the past where a person's decision changes everything. And I wanted to know more about that because she had never really talked to me about that.

JKH: I'm interested in your phrasing there—her "repertoire of stories." [What] you were kind of pushing

against is probably the familiar stories that you had heard and you wanted deeper and—

EK: Well, I didn't know what there was that was deeper yet. But I wanted to know more about *him* and she was kind of [the] easiest way into that. And we did an interview and I was really pushing her for details and stuff, like *give me a little more about this,* going back and asking follow-up questions— different from a conversation with your mother to like the interviewing your mother for the story, but I had to kind of put the compartment down a little bit and act like *You're a source, I'm trying to go back to a historic event and give an eyewitness account of it, a participant's account to it.*

And so we did that and I wrote the essay, and as I was writing the essay and kind of bringing in the details that she gave me but then also what I knew and what I didn't know, I realized that there's still so much now that I don't know [about my father]...He got to die and be a mystery. Whereas if he had lived, I would have grown up and gotten to know him more and probably felt like I knew everything I needed to know about my dad. But my mom just had to continue to be my mother, which is like the most thankless thing in the world. You do get taken for granted, even when you have the razzle-dazzle stories that she has.

But [my starting to ask questions] had a lot to do with also my oldest niece, my mother's oldest grandchild, [who] was about thirteen when I started this project. And I started to think about her.

JKH: **So you're seeing that,** *yeah, she was this age, she was my mother['s age].*

EK: Yeah. I think back to myself at thirteen, and also how I was treated like I was a lot older simply because, like my mother, we were tall...early and that's really all that needs to happen in a lot of ways. But I thought about my niece and she's hyperarticulate. She was an only child for like six years, so she's used to having conversations with adults from an early age. She was thirteen going on thirty, you know. But she was also very unmistakably thirteen. And I started thinking more about that because my Mom's repertoire of stories has included things like, "Well I mean nobody could tell how old I was." And I started to question that.

I always believed that. Because my mother was always an adult since when I can remember. You don't have that concept that like there's a different way that a thirteen-year-old moves through the world. You can tell when a kid is a kid. So then I was like well, let's have more questions about that. Like *how did you end up in New York? How did you get from here to there?* So my mother always told us why she left home was "Well I missed Woodstock in 1969. I didn't want to miss anything else." Which is a great line, isn't it?

JKH: Yes. That's a great line.

EK: But like, *really*? It's a line a thirteen-year-old might have thought, but...that's when I wanted to know: who was the girl who did that? And the things that I thought that I knew about runaways were you run away from home as a kid when it feels safer to be out on your own than it is to be home. And there were none of those hallmarks about my mother's family.

So, Granddaddy was in Vietnam at the time, had volunteered. It was a controversial decision within the family. But it was also a clearer path to promotion up the officer chain. And so he wasn't there—there was an absent father, but it wasn't an absent father that was unexplained. In the army family world [that] had a very clear explanation. There wasn't this sort of abuse or hard neglect or anything beyond the usual mid-century drinking as far as *Mad Men*-style of substance abuse…there wasn't abuse in the home or anything like that. That also made me wonder why.

And that's when I started to think, well, maybe my mother's story is just as interesting as uncovering my father's story. She agreed to do more interviews. She was really generous with her time. And I think maybe she just felt like, well if somebody's finally asking me these questions…She made a decision to be open with me about a lot of things.

JKH: Was she ever trepidatious at any point about her story being told?

EK: So we did all these interviews, and I also did records-diving on my dad and interviewed other family members too [like] her brother (my uncle) and my dad's sister (my aunt)…They knew about the project and were participating in it. And my brother, I had talked to him about it. He was two years older than me, and so [I] could check some of the early memories against his and he would remember things a little more clearly.

JKH: So it was like you had a nest of support.

EK: Yeah. I'm really lucky, my family has always been very supportive of my writing. The way my mother puts in now when she's hyping up my book on Facebook is "To all my friends who have always said I should write a book, I didn't have to. My daughter did it for me." It's a very mom thing to do. But in the end…I said, "I just want to make sure are you still okay with this." And she said, "Well, is it going to hurt anybody?" And I was so stricken by that—that was not what I expected her to say at all.

JKH: How you place that in the book...it really strikes the reader.

EK: After all that, her biggest question was *who is this going hurt?* And from that I really saw the way that she [had been] cast a little bit as the villain of the story by her own parents, who—you know, love my grandparents. She loved them and they reconciled when my brother was a baby and they were always a major part of our lives. But I also saw how she really did spend the rest of their lives...trying to make it up to them [that she had run away]...

But maybe on some level they realized that they had something to make up [for] too. They were all very present in our lives, but I wished for her now that it would've maybe been more explicitly clear that she was the kid who needed to be kept safe, and that kids do these impulsive things sometimes and then decide that they're going to live with it because the world has told them *you make your bed, you lie in it.* That at some point, though, you can rescue them from that.

JKH: One of the things [that resonates about *Runaway*] is how you're telling this story and you have that thread of memoir, you have this cultural element, but [you also] write the detective work, this legwork of the journalist, into this book. We see you writing for arrest records, contacting people. We see you trying to find court records and documents, and bumping up against...the trail [ending]...

How important was it to you to do that, to show that? Because I think a lot of times...people [assume that

memoir is] just flat-out storytelling…a regurgitation of a narrative or whatever, and they don't think that there's research that takes place.

EK: Aside from the journalistic digging, I did do a lot of research to do what my publisher calls "poetic reimaginations" of my mother's time on the road, and I think I was successful in that…doing things from the research like *what color would the squirrels be in the mountains of Colorado?*—that kind of rabbit-hole-y detail we can sometimes do instead of writing but is so fun.

But…I did get some encouragement as I was working on the project overall from some smart writer friends of mine who asked "Where are you in this story?" And I thought, *Well that's a fair question but I'm not very interesting. My mother is interesting, and I am not*…I guess I'm always surprised when people find the work of journalism that's not like *we're busting [the] Harvey Weinstein case wide open* [interesting] because to me it just looks like a lot of grunt work…But I've learned that probably in the way that someone who fishes for a living doesn't necessarily think that their work is the most fascinating, I absolutely want to read the minutiae of like how the lines are set and what it's like when that happens and what it feels like when you bring the catch in.

So I sort of had to get over my sense of *well no one wants to hear about any of that* to go ahead and show the work. But I did also want to *show the work* because…[it's] not the same as writing a novel where you're sort of supposed to generate it all from some magical, imagined space inside of you. And it's not exactly the same as memoir where it's like *well this is my story that I'm gonna bring alive for you.* This kind of hybrid work is just a little different, but I still had to kind of put myself as a character into it.

JKH: What did writing the book reveal to you about yourself?

EK: I was really about halfway through the research and recording before I realized that actually [my mom's] life was a lot more interesting than [my dad's]. I always had a very strong drive, and I do think still that a lot of the reporting that we do along this vein—the drive is to if you can write deeply about the man and figure out why he did the things that he did, then that will suffice in sort of helping everyone wrap their head around whatever the bad thing is that the bad man did. And that then we will feel we can move past it. But I feel like left out of that so often are the women, the girls, whoever.

To use a contemporary example, how many words have we spent on Louis C.K.'s situation, and how hard it is for most people to remember offhand the names of the women that were directly affected? And that's, to me, such a narrative imbalance in the world, and I realize how much—how often I had contributed to that. And I felt bad, I felt sort of terrible. But I also realized that if I can change how I approach these stories—if I can change the stories that I'm looking for also, that I seek out, that I'm drawn to—we can all change these things. They're not static, fixed truths about the universe.

JKH: Where do you hope this book lands right now in terms of our ongoing cultural conversation about this climate of abuse and misogyny?

EK: I want there to be more conversations about *I was wrong about this,* because I do feel like we don't quite make enough space for that. It's almost like maybe you need to sit in the corner and think about what you've done or what you haven't done enough of instead of giving us enough space to talk about how our thinking has evolved, how we have changed.

Because people are going to progress. Progress, it's never fast enough, that's just the truth. But I don't think it necessarily pushes progress more effectively to try and speed past people and not let them make their own decisions and come to their own way of thinking. You hope that it's in a timely fashion and they aren't harming people in the meantime. But I do hope that it opens up more of a conversation about *this is a thing that's also happening all around you all the time.*

There's really nothing inherently special about Harvey Weinstein, [it's] just because we know his name. He had outsized cultural influence, but within every community, there's guys like that [who] have outsized cultural influence locally...and Harvey Weinstein is as much of a product of the culture as he was a purveyor of the culture. So that way when we say, *well how many people let this happen?*—that is always the question. How many people had to look the other way? How many assistants just signed the NDA and took the payout? How many movie execs were all too happy to let the rumors fly? I feel like then we all have to kind of take a step back and say *well, how many people let this local quote-unquote "scandal" happen?*

The answer is a lot of people have to not necessarily even actively look the other way, they just have to buy into the idea that a man's comfort and standing is more important than harm against a woman, a child, anybody with less power...

When people are like *I've been canceled,* it's like, *I think you're fine.* You know? But the loss of status for important men is seen as a death. And that's what I would hope is this book has a place in the conversation about how do we actually talk about loss of status in a way other than actual death? Because it's not the same. We shouldn't be treating it as the same...

We're in the middle of [a] pretty strong backlash right now to #MeToo. And I think it's because we maybe didn't sit enough with *what is this like in our local and personal communities?* in a way that could actually affect change. I mean, you see plenty of social media callouts, but what is the work that we're all doing? I think a lot of people just sort of don't know what to do. I don't know what to do either—I mean I didn't write a field guide or anything for it.

But I'm generally of the feeling that the more you talk openly about things, even the things that you might have made a mistake on or even been culpable in, if you can just be open and honest about it with the spirit of *can we try to fix things?* then that's good. Progress can happen in those moments too. ■

INTERVENTION

History museum's
banner outside reads:

*The world reflected
through complex*

cultural histories.
Sabra and Shatilla.

Shays Rebellion.
Work hands, wind

ruffling brows, sand
slipping from eyes.

No fixed thing,
immeasurable light,

underside of air.

ADAM DAY

PLAYING A PART

In the room
where always

another has been
with an old oar

pushing the waves
away in a sea

of sleet.

ADAM DAY

PASSING STOREFRONTS

Common army
eating earth, refracting

light. History
depending on proximity

to power, the body.
Egret nested

in the moon;
trees run out

of breath
or the winds

beat them back.

ADAM DAY

THIRSTY HEAT

Words are not quite
words, so we can talk,

or fall asleep head
to feet after quarry

diving, spitting
blood and water

between our teeth.

ADAM DAY

WOOD THRUSHES

Flushed women come
from a hedge gap

detaching from light
skirts clinging twigs.

They smoke
staring at the red

neck of a lightning bug,
and a live oak above.

ADAM DAY

DAY
SEVEN

MELISSA HELTON

It's been a week. And I don't know what to say. It is so big.

I can say it is three a.m. and my cat inexplicably woke me up at the same time that I stirred on July 28th, feeling queasy and uncomfortable enough that I sat up in bed in the dark, wondering if I needed a Tums, wondering if I was going to be sick, wondering why I felt so terrible. And then

I looked at my phone, which was silently blowing up with missed calls, texts, and messages. I did not go back to sleep. I can't this morning either.

I can give a record of events. How in the preceding days I had been in the joy of the forty-fifth annual Appalachian Writers' Workshop, the first fully in-person workshop since the pandemic began. I had finished leading the Troublesome Team Trivia contest and driven home instead of staying on campus that night. So when the flood hit in the wee hours of that Thursday morning, I was able to act as remote communication, spending a literal eleven hours on my phone. I began relaying information across campus from an hour away since I had one contact with cell service in each of the four areas where the workshop writers were stranded by the flood water. Then arranging rides home for those whose cars had washed away or were four feet underwater, relaying road condition information, answering the concerns of writers not on campus. I can tell you how those eleven hours were filled with fear and then joy as I learned all my friends, teachers, mentors, and fellow writers were safe on and off campus, and managed to eventually make it home.

I can talk about my first view of campus on Friday. The disorientation of book tables still set up for the remaining days of the writers' workshop in one place, and broken glass, splintered wood, upended desks, and flood mud in others. The donations. The distribution. The crying community members who lost everything, or lost nothing and were heartbroken for others. The calls and texts and emails and social media posts and questions and best-guess decisions and donations and meals and stunned faces and hugs from strangers and mud and old photos and meals and water bottles and questions and questions and a few hours' sleep at night to do it again for a week straight.

I can talk about being in charge of saving our archive. Ninety-five percent of the material was wet, seventy percent of it also covered in mud. Books, handwritten records, photos, quilts, baskets, files, silver nitrate negatives—precious historical items significant to us and the Appalachian region.

I can describe standing there in the archive, my two teenagers sweeping the dark scene with flashlights as we sloshed through three-inch putrid mud, and how it was so big a disaster I didn't know where to start, completely unqualified for such an important and time-sensitive task. And how that feeling has not gone away this entire week as we've hurried to do what we could. And the list of names and organizations who have emailed me advice, websites and tutorials, came on site for hours or days, helped pull materials from the molding rooms, helped make these sometimes educated and sometimes uneducated decisions, arranged for transport of documents or offered their freezer space for preservation—it's a long list. If I began naming people and organizations, for each one I could pull forth here, I would forget at least six. Some names I never got in the first place. Our Great Hall became our supply distribution center and is also a working archive rescue center. Tables of diapers and garbage bags sit across from clotheslines of irreplaceable photos and slides slowly drying as folks hurry back and forth. And the only reason these items are being rescued is because of these volunteers.

I can say how everyone has been thrust into positions where they are scrambling to learn what needs done and how to do it, and are moving mountains to get the needed work done. I usually work on creative writing and gardening programming in the schools. Our staff have become social workers and FEMA liaisons. My teenagers are becoming donation distribution managers and junior archivists. Folks are volunteering in the kitchen to help feed whoever shows up needing to eat, and doing so in a situation without normal things like running potable water, a working freezer, or gas for the stoves. Homeowners are learning flood reclamation. Churches and the Sportsplex are emergency centers, and elementary schools are military barracks. We are all grief counselors.

I can write about the emotional impact, how confusing and bizarre it is to be completely heartbroken and heart-filled at the exact same moment. I wouldn't compare it to a roller coaster. Those, we can see where we are going to a large extent. We can know we are building up to a big drop or an upside-down flip or a water splash down. This situation is like bumper cars in the dark with strobe lights on. We don't see what is about to sideswipe or jar us. If we do, we see it right before it hits without time to prepare. One second, I am holding the hand of a stranger as they say, "We lost everything, absolutely everything, but we're okay because we all got out" and I am trying to grasp that *that* is the bar—we are okay because no one is dead.

That is this crisis's definition of okay.

And then a volunteer pops their head in the door and shouts we have nineteen pallets of donated water bottles that need unloaded. Then after catching my breath, a text dings through in my pocket to say some angel is rushing down from central Kentucky, or over from Virginia, or up from Tennessee to help clean archive documents or bring a trailer load of food and toiletries or help pull debris from a building. As I'm responding to that text, I hear a screech up on the hill and see a displaced child, whose family lost their home and is staying on campus. She is swinging on our rope in her pajamas and squealing in delight. And I hold that simple joy in the foreground for a second, then I think of all her family lost and is struggling through right now. Then I think of a child in our dyslexia program who died. Then I hear someone laughing into their phone because his dog has been found alive. Then a now-homeless ninety-four-year-old woman is telling me on the porch how she's never seen a flood like this in her life and she doesn't know where to go and she remembers attending maypole dances here, on that grass, eighty-five years ago. Then three guys from West Virginia roll up and offer to cook burgers for everyone and they have everything they need so we don't have to worry about providing the community supper tonight. Then a donation truck. Then the water cuts off again. Then a friend texts: "I know you're swamped. You don't need to respond to this. Just know I'm thinking of you and let me know if you need anything." Then a report the death toll has risen. Then, then, then, then.

I am trying to grasp that that *is the bar—we are okay because no one is dead. That is this crisis's definition of okay.*

Slammed in every other direction every other moment. And then a colleague asks *have you taken a break, have you eaten yet, have you had some water?* They ask "how are you" and you just look at them and say "yeah." And they know because it's the same for them. And there's nothing really that can be said to hold something this big.

I can say how several times a day there will be a pressure valve release that causes a mini-breakdown. Seeing emergency archive documentation in my thirteen-year-old's handwriting. Cry. Watching my sixteen-year-old pause from breaking down cardboard boxes to greet a stunned community member at the door, to point to where they can get a hot meal, explain where they can find cleaning supplies to take home. Cry. A message from my momma, eighty-years-old and 500 miles away, texting me that so-and-so responded to my Facebook post and did I call them yet, it seems important, here is their number. Cry. Seeing a perfume bottle made by my late father, a glassblower, lifted from the mud of my former office in the hand of someone from a volunteer crew, unbroken. Cry.

Little moments where everything high up under the surface of my heart can crack through and release a bit. Then wiping tears on my shirt sleeve and doing the next task.

I can write about the anger and fear for our region, how extractive industries are a huge accomplice in these tragedies—not only environmentally but also in creating a world that made outsiders rich off our bodies and mountains and left us with a much-needed restructuring of our local and regional economies. In the interim, many in our counties were barely making it. And now the little security we had built is gone. This boils up a rage at industry and politicians. And we know, in the coming disasters, the rich will have what they need: water, food, ability to flee. They always do. It's the poor that will suffer the most and die. That's how it's always been. Cast your vote in November...do what you can in your own life...and it's not changing fast enough. And I listen to a mud-splattered man explain how they're the only one who can get out of their holler and they're needing supplies and food for five households, and I know the next 100-year flood will be here much sooner than 100 years and the people making the decisions that are creating most of this crisis aren't the ones that will suffer the consequences.

I can admit how after a week of this deluge I am simultaneously bone-weary exhausted, and wired and can't sit still. During an *I'm gonna sit for ten minutes and rest* break, I will suddenly find that, as I've been responding to calls, texts, and emails, I have stood up and I'm rocking foot to foot and I don't remember getting up out of the chair.

I can say my brain is mush. Names and words are elusive and hard to pull forth. I forgot our director Will's name yesterday and took eight seconds to recover it, which seems a long time to remember someone's name you work with every day. I find myself staring into space having forgotten what I was about to go do. Writing this piece has been a Herculean effort here in the dark while my family sleeps and my Earl Grey cools. I'm sure these are all typical experiences in such situations. We have hired more support staff and as the archive emergency ends in the coming days, my schedule will become more sustainable. Right now, there is not much time to rest.

My throat is sore from speaking so much.

I can say how honored I am to work with these people, to see how they rise up to help others while they are hurting and reeling themselves. Their efforts and care are tremendous. And I am honored to work at Hindman Settlement School which is doing such needful work, as it always has through its 120-year history.

I can say I wish I could list all those I owe a thanks to.

I can say I am thankful for my husband, helping to pull things from the mud, packing the car with supplies and morning coffee, sending texts through the day saying *I love you, I'm proud of you*, curling me into his arms at the end of the day and finding a YouTube video about growing indeterminate cucumbers in a high tunnel to distract my mind and heart from the flood for a few minutes.

I can say I probably should've stayed in bed this morning, that I most likely would've drifted back off and gotten another hour of rest, and I know I'll be extra tired today on just four hours of sleep, but I needed to write this, and we have plenty of caffeine on campus. This fatigue is temporary.

I can say all the deeply true clichés: This recovery will be a marathon and not a sprint. Our community has been brought together by this. There are no divisions of religion or politics but just a mutual aid and care—no one offering me help or asking me for help cares what my sexual orientation is or what I think about kneeling during the national anthem. We are a community that says if we haven't lost a loved one, everything else is suddenly less important than it was eight days ago. We are a community that says we are blessed even as we stand amidst destruction and loss and fear, that we need nothing in return for our money, our labor, our time, our donations, our care, that we are just happy to be able to help.

I'm just happy to be able to help.

I'm so, so happy I've been able to help.

And now it's six-thirty a.m. I need to pack up my mud boots and get back in the car. ▮

AUGURING A MIDNIGHT FIELD

One

Surprising the stars,
a red-winged blackbird bursts up—
not as drunk as I.

Two

Candles, thread, six signs:
the farmhouse has yellow eyes,
owling the gaunt dark.

Three

Sidestepping horseshit,
I follow headlong the path
lit by the bare moon.

Four

Whiskey gone, night's twin
never arrives. My mind is
several parts of stone.

GABRIEL DUNSMITH

BASEBALL

find myself walking
       to the baseball field   warm
             on the hill
to spot a former, paper self

You know The Field. The Field with the
parking spot fan etched beyond the fence
                  thefencethatwas
chain link, summer term dressings
that strong kids would moon fastballs over
                itwaslemmethink
yielding eucalyptus saloon doors
past worm-burner bullpens, extra grass
where dogs long dead played tireless fetch.

when Subaru windshields shattered in view
dugout riot while the parents heeled around
to their bleacher-bum friends like "whose car? whose car?"
the owner would shrug like "it's baseball, what can you do?"

expecting lemon-tonic sun but it's shadows folding over
from the pines and musky eucalyptus trunk
stunning nevermind from a sallow sky
since so many kids drunk their gatorades dry

Townspeople hurry their dogs, teenage bikes
rattle by in ridicule, getting callous
for some battle surely behind the bend
maybe wonder why a man stands in shallow center
worrying a time pressed in archival amber

ELAN MAIER

ON GRAFTON, WEST VIRGINIA IN THE FALL

KIRSTEN RENEAU

After James Agee's "Knoxville: Summer of 1915"

I am thinking now of the autumn evenings in West Virginia, a time and place I have come to believe I will never visit again. I once lived on a hill near town where trees stood over our house, which was light brown with dark trim and was always warm with a fire going, upstairs and down. There was a spacious side yard which held a doghouse for Tonya, a perfectly average mutt who couldn't be contained by a fence and instead spent her afternoons tied up the tree, napping in the wooden home my father made her. The back yard was a slope made up mostly of trees, tall trees that stood watch over the homes always in varying shades and states of loss. The trees stood so tall you had to step back to see their tops and had just begun to turn over to the whims of nature, fading into fall's colors of reds, oranges, yellows, and greens. There was the woodshed, of course, where my father spent his free time, and the house he made for us to play in, a replica of our home. The house proper was trimmed with bushes and flowers passed down from the previous owner. My family was never any good at keeping plants, but the yard around the house was always bright and alive no matter the season.

But it's autumn I wish to speak about; specifically, the moment where afternoon became evening and earth turned golden. The air was still warm but carried a promise of a chill soon in the air; inside, my mother was beginning to pull out red sweaters and heavy blue coats that we'd soon need for the mornings of the cold front to come. Standing in my front yard and facing out, the hills had turned the color of wheat as the sun lowered itself, and above the hills the sky was fading to grey, the first few stars of Pisces beginning to bloom. The forest that bled into the fields and hills was beginning to lose its edges as piles of leaves started to gather around the tree trunks, which were dark and held initials carved from some long-ago lovers. The air smelled clean. There was the sound of bugs awakening, the crickets playing along to the guitar heard through a window somewhere down the street.

As the light continued to fade, the fireflies started to become restless and tried to make themselves into stars. From the forest, I could see a deer emerge. It was a doe; she dipped her head and nibbled on the grass. It was not rare necessarily, but it was a certain indicator of the movement of the season, that the deer had begun to run out of grass within their homes between the trees. There was no way she could hear me, but I held my breath just in case. There were no cars, no train whistles in the background; it was both too early and too late for those sounds, and instead we were offered the easy voices of nature, which made the space and time feel electric, like a promise. ■

FICTIVE
DREAMIN'

JAKE MAYNARD

How often do writers dream about writing? I'm thinking about the physical act: ass + chair, furrowed squint, eyelid quaking, temple tap and chewed lips. The keyboard chatters. *Writing.*

I've been wondering because it finally happened to me. I've been writing hard for maybe six years and finally some pages appeared in my dreams. Maybe it took so long because the act of writing, at least as I practice it, is pretty bleh. It's mostly sitting and thinking and walking to the window and drawing dicks in the fogged glass. Sometimes the good words come, and sometimes they don't. Despite writers' thirst for narrative, the act itself doesn't have a particularly compelling one. Writers' angst, at best, is melodrama—a little like the tangles of bodies and naked TED talks that haunt me while I sleep.

I texted some writer friends about it:

Meredith: Maybe once every other month? I feel like I get good ideas in my dreams but never remember them when I wake up. Or my dreams are like 'make characters go mini-golfing.'

Me: So are you actively writing in these dreams?

Meredith: Sometimes. They usually start with me getting feedback and feeling like I need to change something so I'm never straight up writing in my dreams.

Randi: I used to dream about getting awesome story ideas and either I could not remember them when I woke up or they turned out to be trash in reality. Sometimes I dreamed about my books selling. Mostly I dream about solving mysteries or running from murderers and terrorists or junk like that.

Noelle: No, but I did practice Chinese in a dream the other day.

Whit: I don't think I do. I'll dream about work emails sometime, but most of the dreams are fast-paced, moving screenplays. Plot twist. Revelation. Very movie-like. Me jumping out of bed like a lunatic about once a month, turning the light on, thinking there's a dead snake—or something like that—in my sheets. Me panting, confused but coming to, slowly realizing it's all a dream.

■ ■ ■

Hardly a reliable sample size, but research suggests writing as a physical act rarely makes the dreamscape. This makes me wonder what John Gardner would say about it. If writing prose is itself a kind of dream-state—he called it the fictive dream—dreaming about it becomes outright lasagnal.

In *The Art of Fiction*, Gardner writes:

> *In the writing state—the state of inspiration—the fictive dream springs up fully alive: the writer forgets the words he has written on the page and sees, instead, his characters moving around their rooms, hunting through cupboards, glancing irritably through their mail, setting mousetraps, loading pistols. The dream is as alive and compelling as one's dreams at night, and when the writer writes down on paper what he has imagined, the words, however inadequate, do not distract his mind from the fictive dream but provide him with a fix on it, so that when the dream flags he can reread what he's written and find the dream starting up again.*

Here, Gardner's talking specifically about the fictive dream as the writer experiences it, but the term has grown to refer to the continuous state of immersion that you feel inside of good fiction. In a workshop, God Forbid, you might hear, "that part on page three with the bullet points breaks the dream."

Gruff, smug, and intimidating in an academic white-guy sort of way, Gardner's the type of writer most folks read once as they start out, then not again. He died in a motorcycle accident in 1984 at age forty-nine, three days before his third wedding—tragedy stalked his family; a farm accident had horrifically killed his brother, leaving Gardner with lifelong nightmares—but his short life was prolific to the tune of twenty-five books. His Beowulf retelling, *Grendel*, got the most contemporary attention, but *The Art of Fiction* might be the more important work.

That quote pops up on every other newbie writing advice blog, giving a hip term and some philosophical underpinning to the largely ambiguous act that early writers are working to understand. It's interesting that in *The Art of Fiction*, the fictive dream is just a guiding idea, intended to help readers move through the more specific craft stuff that follows. But his guiding idea is remembered more than the corollary writing tips.

Just like a dream, the specifics fade but the feeling loiters.

■ ■ ■

So, we write what we dream, and we dream what we write, but we rarely dream that we write. And writing is itself a dream-state, at least when it's going well, and so is reading, at least when it's going well. But my fiction teachers taught me to never dramatize dreams, the allegation being that dreams are only interesting to the dreamer.

But—

It started with a young couple struggling to maintain a spa at the site of some hot springs in remote interior Alaska. The caretaker's name was Bogdan, and marauding bears, attracted by the vegetation that grew near the springs, were Bogdan's antagonist. He had to stay up late to keep the bears away so that couples could fuck in the springs. The lodge owners' marriage was failing and Bogdan was caught in the middle, not explicitly sexually but maybe a little sexually. And if they split, would he lose his job?

It was shaping up to be a usable dream, but before the penultimate conflict, I was sucked from the world of the spa with a whacky rabbit-hole logic. I found myself looking at a Microsoft Word document with the story written on it. Something like: *Each night, while the guests ate their crab legs, Bogdan walked the grounds blowing an airhorn into the woods to spook the bears.*

It was like I had moved from a movie to its script and missed nothing.

I stood from the computer and was suddenly outside in a suburb of Anchorage that was also my hometown in rural Pennsylvania. It was a bluebird day. Someone was mowing a lawn. I walked down the street—now it looked more like Pittsburgh—and I saw the mailman trying to steal my laptop.

But dissection can only get us so far. Parsing out a dream's influences doesn't really explain it, in the same way that picking out writers' strategies doesn't explain the magic of reading great work.

(This was right after the 2020 election). I rushed him and pushed him down and learned that it wasn't the mailman at all but an editor. My novel-in-progress was open on the screen. He said I used way too many em dashes.

It wasn't hard to suss it out. That night, I'd been messing with my novel, which is set in Alaska, and thinking about this hot spring in the Yukon I'd visited where some bathers were recently mauled. Bogdan was the name of an NBA player I'd been watching. My girlfriend was moving to Pittsburgh and would I go with her? And the em dashes—I'd just counted the number of times I'd used the words fuck (272), motherfucker

(39), jerk off (16), and the phrase "fuck piss shit" (7) in my novel draft, out of worry that the book was too vulgar.

But dissection can only get us so far. Parsing out a dream's influences doesn't *really* explain it, in the same way that picking out writers' strategies doesn't explain the magic of reading great work. What I mean is that 272 motherfuckers aren't inherently too few or too many. It's easy to forget that, though, especially when it feels like the key to becoming a good fiction writer is to demystify how fiction works. Unfortunately, *craft* can't collate your data.

In graduate school, deep in craft, there were times that I forgot how to read fiction, which is to say I lost the ability to experience the fictive dream. Instead, I tried to atomize Lorrie Moore and study the dust in the window light. Aleksandar Hemon, Percival Everett, Toni Morrison, Halldór Laxness—I stalked my favorite texts with a scalpel, thinking I could hack away pieces and recombine them into something that moves.

Four years removed, and I'm learning to dream on the page again.

■ ■ ■

The first time I can remember experiencing the deep dream of reading was in the fifth grade. The book was an abridged version of Shelley's *Frankenstein*, which Shelley first envisioned in a dream. Towards the end, as the story moves through fast summaries, Victor chases his monster across Europe. *I pursued him... Guided by a slight clue, I followed the windings of the Rhone, but vainly. The blue Mediterranean appeared, and by a strange chance, I saw the fiend enter by night and hide himself in a vessel bound for the Black Sea. I took my passage in the same ship, but he escaped, I know not how.*

I was too young to get the creator/creation metaphor back then, but I still followed Victor through the Russian countryside as he tracked his monster/shadow-self/artwork. Consumed with hate, it's only when sleeping that Victor *could taste joy...During the day I was sustained and inspirited by the hope of night, for in sleep I saw my friends, my wife, and my beloved country.*

Victor's sense of reality flutters, thinking that he is *dreaming until night should come and that I should then enjoy reality in the arms of my dearest friends.* The monster, always out of sight, mocks him, carving messages onto trees, beckoning Victor towards his certain death on the frozen seas to the North. Finally, on the ice, Victor *sees a dark speck upon the dusky plain. I strained my sight to discover what it could be and uttered a wild cry of ecstasy when I distinguished a sledge and the distorted proportions of a well-known form within. Oh! With what a burning gush did hope revisit my heart!*

The sea ice heaves and buckles, his enemy escapes, and Victor, *thus preparing* for his *hideous death*, realizes that his journey has not been of his own will. *Oh! When will my guiding spirit, in conducting me to the dæmon, allow me the rest I so much desire; or must I die, and he yet live?... He is eloquent and persuasive, and once his words had even power over my heart; but trust him not...*

Just then some shithead sneezed and the words became words, nothing more than weird little runes. No dusky plain, no ice, no glowworm of ship light in the distance. Ink on paper—flat, yellowed, and smelling just a little like catpiss. I remember feeling almost scared when I scanned the classroom and saw big-eared CJ Miller wiping his nose with his sleeve to my left. My body had been right next to him, but a part of me was someplace else.

For a few years after that, I dreamed that I was driving a team of sled dogs through a whiteout, chasing something. It was only when I started writing fiction that I had the feeling again.

■ ■ ■

I felt it again years later, reading Mary Ann Samyn's poem "Beneath Speech." It begins:
She lay very still, looking up at the undersides of words.
That was it.
That was the sensation.
Gardner's dream, distilled.
But no one explains it as well as Julio Cortázar in *The Continuity of Parks,* in which the main character sits down with a book and slips into a narrative of a woman and her lover at a secret meeting. *Word by word, immersed in the sordid dilemma of the hero and heroine, letting himself go toward where the images came together and took on color and movement, he was witness to the final encounter in the mountain cabin.*

The subtext says murder. *The dagger warmed itself against his chest, and underneath pounded liberty, ready to spring.* The scene of the man reading and the scene that he reads begin to intertwine. *A lustful, yearning dialogue raced down the pages like a rivulet of snakes.* Following a series of parks, the man with the dagger makes for the city and sneaks into the fine estate of his victim. He knows from his lover where to find the man, and when he enters the correct room he sees *the high back of an armchair covered in green velvet, the head of the man in the chair reading a novel.*

Right?!

The undergrads I teach go apeshit for *Parks*. With some prodding, they notice that the parks and the green velvet chair—think: nature, natural cycles, whatever—connect the novel to the lived life. More than a clever metafictional commentary on art, Cortázar makes fictive play deeply moving. The main character actually reads his life as it unfolds to him, which sounds a lot like Joan Didion's "we tell ourselves stories in order to live."

Gardner, again: "discovering the meaning and communicating the meaning are for the writer one single act." Cortázar and Didion tell us the same thing. The relationship between the writer and their work is recursive. Our work is simultaneously made *and* revealed through the making. It's the kind of tasty mystery that no craft book can explain. It's the kind of mystery we ought to respect.

■ ■ ■

It's not hard to see similarities between Cortázar's man in the green velvet chair and Victor Frankenstein. They both lose track of the line between dream and waking life, and they both forget that the meaning is revealed as it is made, and not before. The man in the chair, too focused on his work and his book, sees his estranged wife and her lover as harmless, while Victor's primary issue is also of fixed perspective. When Victor looks at his creation, he sees a failed attempt at a man and not a kickass monster. Victor forgets that the magic of art is the unknowableness, and the ensuing rough fumbling and searching. (In fairness, his creation does murder his best buddy and fiancée, while the work of most writers just alienates their parents.)

If writing is turning "world into word," like Mark Doty says, the dreams of a writer can show us how imperfect the process can be. In my dream at the hot springs, I was incepted with all of the requisite context: the troubles between the owners, Bogdan's name, his backstory—everything I need to know flooded my perception, like a vein was opened, as soon as the dream began. The real unbelievability was that it could be transferred so seamlessly to script.

What I mean is that maybe dreams matter so much to the artist because they inspire *and* humble. They show us what's possible, and remind us what's not.

■ ■ ■

Lately I have been trying to respect the ineffability of writing and reading and dreaming, which might explain why I keep thinking about John Gardner and listening to a dead country singer named Townes Van Zandt. Van Zandt wrote witty and surreal narratives about love, landscape, and addiction. As a teen in the early 1960s, supposedly suffering from bipolar disorder, he was given insulin shock therapy in a psychiatric ward in Texas, a procedure which put him in short comas regularly over many weeks. (Insulin shock therapy, which Sylvia Plath writes about in *The Bell Jar*, is widely discredited.) In interviews, Van Zandt said that he had no memories of his childhood. It makes sense, given all those comas and no memories to pull from, that he would fixate on dreams. In that way, Van Zandt was the opposite of Gardner: one haunted by his past, the other haunted by his lack of it.

When Van Zandt dramatizes a dream, the language dissolves alongside the waking logic. In "When You Dream Lovers Die," he sings,

"When your sky starts to tumble / and your rhymes starts to lose / The meaning so tenderly given / When all your dreams lie down and die at your shoes / You can turn to me for livin'... And now you must follow your dreams as they fly / Leaving trails of empty feeling / Perhaps when you watch all your dream lovers die / You'll decide that you need a real one."

I love the way that the dreams leave you unfulfilled, yet resolved. The way that dreams humble *and* inspire.

Similarly, "Lungs": "Fingers walk the darkness down / Mind is on the midnight / Gather up the gold you've found / You fool, it's only moonlight / And if you stop to take it home / Your hands will turn to butter / Better leave this dream alone / Try to find another."

Van Zandt didn't talk much about his artistic process, and for that I'm glad. But in the 1976 documentary *Heartworn Highways*, he does give us a little insight. In the kitchen of his singlewide outside Nashville, surrounded by whisky bottles, outcast friends, and busted furniture, Townes introduces a song by saying: "This is one I wrote about two Mexican bandits that I saw on the TV, two weeks after I wrote the song."

I used to think it was just a dumb joke.

But now I think I'm starting to see.

He's telling us how it happens. ■

REMEMBERING PANDEMIC TEACHING

My students comment on the new bookshelf
in my Zoom background.
It lives below my framed diploma,
a print of *The Persistence of Memory*
and a half-visible, beveled mirror.

A peer told me I looked "put together"
when Zooming, but
no one can see the immediacy
of the kitchen sink on my right,
the bulging sectional to my left,
hovering so near the frame, I must turn
to pass between it and the desk I teach at.
They cannot hear my failing marriage haunt the house.

Even in this state, though,
I keep up pretenses,
keep the sink and couch at bay,
turn my mind from my marriage.
But these things press in, camera hungry.
My darting eyes grow weary
from begging them for peace.

How many others lived such weariness?
All I saw were half-lives at the edges of screens:
unfinished artwork, severed bookcases, cat tails,
family members passing in and out like ghosts.

RACHEL BATES

DIVORCÉE DATING

At an Italian restaurant in the West Village,
my date thought I said I divorced my husband
and have "four kids" instead of "before kids."
I lauded his suppressed shock
but noted his sheer surprise
through a spaghettied mouthful repetition of "four kids?!"
suddenly more thankful than ever
I left when I did.

RACHEL BATES

BOOK REVIEWS

Jordan Farmer. *The Poison Flood.* **New York, N.Y.: G.P. Putnam's Sons , 2020. 288 pages. Hardcover. $26.00.**

Reviewed by Randi Adams

Through the first-person narration of Hollis Bragg, guitarist and secret songwriter for a popular mainstream band, Jordan Farmer presents a story of murder, environmental destruction, music, love, and identity. *The Poison Flood*, Farmer's second novel, is hyperfocused on a week-long string of events that take place in a small West Virginia town. Hollis's unique perspective is informed largely by the  outsider status he has incurred due to his hunched back. The plot of the novel lurches forward when Hollis's self-inflicted reclusivity is shattered by a fan and an environmentalist zealot just as a chemical spill leaves the county's water poisoned and the region in crisis. The dangers Hollis faces in relation to the contamination and the violent fallout force him to reckon with his sense of self, his relationships with women, and the isolation and anonymity he has been hiding within.

As is common in Appalachian literature, The Poison Flood exhibits a self-awareness of Appalachia's role in American consciousness. Hollis, unsurprised by the lack of aid following the contamination, tells the reader, "In many ways, we've always been on our own, addressed only when the rest of the country requires our resources or needs something to mock." Farmer expertly parallels this exploitation on a micro-level as we see the county, full of people who have mythologized Hollis as a monster, come to rely on him for his unspoiled well water. It is a poignant metaphor for a cruel and all-too-true reality. In some of his most beautiful prose, Farmer continually links Hollis's body with place, furthering this metaphor.

The novel's most obvious antagonist is essentially an eco-terrorist which creates a dramatic sense of tension within the narrative given the plot is largely driven by an environmental disaster. It is an interesting choice by Farmer, who could have easily given the story a perfect martyr. Instead, via Victor's violent zeal, Farmer asks the reader to interrogate their own sense of right and wrong. Yet Victor falls flat as a character. Perhaps he is too much; a voyeuristic and explosive persona in a uniform of a cowboy hat and spurs. Or perhaps he is not enough; with almost no background story, his zeal seems unearned at times. Victor's believability especially falters in comparison to the novel's other malicious extremist, Hollis's father–the Reverend. Victor becomes a caricature of a villain, almost to the point of the unbelievable, making it difficult to see him as a true threat.

While the novel is, on the surface, crime noir with an environmental consciousness, at its heart, it is a love story and a reckoning with identity. Music is a driving force for Hollis, but at an early stage in his life, it is secondary. He begins making music because of and for Angela, whom he meets as a teenager. The pair bond over guitar lessons and Angela becomes Hollis's escape from his abusive father and from the loneliness he faces. Music becomes a larger part of his identity later in life, after he leaves The Troubadours, the band he and Angela founded. Hollis derives much of his self-worth through his relationships with women—Angela, Caroline, and eventually, Rosita, using music as a means to foster these relationships. Even in catastrophe, even in potentially fatal situations, Hollis's mind returns to the women in his life, his relationships with them, and their considerations of his body, or what he imagines as their considerations. In the most dire situations, Hollis ultimately wants to be desired and loved—something to which everyone can connect. It is in these moments, Hollis's most vulnerable admissions, that Farmer's candid, honest, and, surprisingly, tender storytelling functions at its best.

Hollis's relationship with his disabled body is in a continuous state of change. While it does lean toward resentment and apathy, Farmer makes it clear that perfect acceptance of one's physical body is less important than rejecting Hollis's brand of self-hatred and self-pity. These emotions keep Hollis in solitude and prevent him from performing his music and accepting any form of love or intimacy from women, or any measure of kindness from anyone else, for that matter. The closest Hollis gets to praising his body is when he is contemplating how he uses it to make music. Early in the narrative, while strumming a guitar, Farmer writes, "My fingers [prove] they are the only part of my body that hasn't betrayed me. While the rest of my genes are hell-bent on destroying themselves, my hands feel noble grasping the rosewood neck." Hollis is unable to see his body in a positive way as it relates to love and sex, but does see its power in the creation of music.

Hollis's journey to finally moving on from Angela and establishing an identity of his own hinges, in large part, on his desire to preserve his solo project—to attach himself, his name, his body, to a creative legacy. Hollis's project, the concept album he refers to as "the wasteland lullabies" has a narrative structure reminiscent of McCarthy's The Road. Two travelers, the troubadour and the boy, find one another in a post-apocalyptic wasteland, and the man tries to teach the boy some unspecified lesson through his guitar. Toward the end of the novel, Hollis describes the creation of a song for this project: "Luminous music swirls inside my head until all of creation is smothered by song." The description of the creative energy in this scene is perhaps the brightest and most hope-filled of the novel. While Farmer never reveals in any definitive way what the troubadour is trying to teach the boy, a lesson of hope seems fitting.

In this lesson is the hope that sees Hollis emerging from isolation, performing music again, and even approaching the possibilities of romantic relationship. There's a happiness to the ending that satisfies the arc of the underdog, while also bucking the tradition of the modern inspirational feel-good tale, in part due to Farmer's unflinching prose. ■

MONTH-END RITUAL ON MISSISSIPPI TITLE APPLICATION

The corner office

frosted glass grandma chose

when she built the dealership
Seven Styrofoam cups hold

veils the oak desk donated by Christians.
ghost pepper whiskey so combustible

rubber cowboys drink and boast with tongues afire until

shredding time
dead deals
ole buddies

head knockers
knuckle blood
prayers

rooftop keys
roaches
land yachts

small fortunes
distinct knocks
scooped trades
grains of salt

become constellation
truth of our asphalt
lot by the eastside canal
    where police shoot
        sunset cottonmouths
            coiled on sandbanks while

September books balance.

ADDISON GRIFFIS

BUSINESS TOOL ON ODOMETER STATEMENT

Per father's advice,

A pen stays

On my person. He once compared its value,
Match-light in a cave, while I scrubbed
Diesel from my palms, and rainbows
Swirled on hose-water runoff after
I quit warehouse work.

Now ballpoint and fingernail pressure
Imprint on carbon paper contracts
Like spurs and oat barrel on the rubber
Floor of my tack room, pine walls
Adorned with bent iron shoes
Of Quarter Horses, broken.

ADDISON GRIFFIS

CONTRIBUTORS

Randi Adams received her Master of Arts in English from Western Carolina University. She has presented at the American Literature Association and Appalachian Studies conferences, among others, and her essay, "Corpse Birds and Cooling Boards: Appalachian Death Ways in Ron Rash's Short Stories," is published in the *Journal of the Short Story in English*. She is most interested in Southern and Appalachian literature and cultural history, especially in relation to economic class and the environment.

Rachel Bates is an Appalachian poet and English doctoral student living and teaching in Knoxville, Tennessee. She studies Contemporary Appalachian literature against environmental and cultural frameworks, as well as considering Appalachian futures both academically and creatively. Her poetry has appeared in *Gravel, West Texas Literary Review*, and *Broad River Review*, and among other publications.

Adam Day is the author of *Left-Handed Wolf* (LSU Press), and of *Model of a City in Civil War* (Sarabande Books), and the recipient of a Poetry Society of America Chapbook Fellowship for *Badger, Apocrypha*, and of a PEN Award. His work has appeared in the *APR, Boston Review, The Progressive, Volt, Kenyon Review, Iowa Review*, and elsewhere. He is the publisher of *Action, Spectacle*.

Gabriel Dunsmith's poems and environmental essays have appeared in *Poetry, Tikkun, On the Seawall, The Guardian*, and *Grist*. Originally from Asheville, North Carolina, he lives in Reykjavík, Iceland.

Lynn Gilbert has had poems in *Blue Unicorn, Concho River Review, Exquisite Corpse, Gnu, The Huron River Review, Kansas Quarterly, Light, Mezzo Cammin, Mortar, Peninsula Poets*, and *The Texas Observer*, among publications. She was a founding editor of *Borderlands: Texas Poetry Review* and a finalist in the Gerald Cable Book Award in 2021. She helps edit *Third Wednesday* literary magazine.

Addison Griffis is a Mississippi writer and finance manager at a car dealership. He writes prose and poetry between deals. Griffis is currently querying his third manuscript for publication and working on various recording projects in his barn/studio.

Melissa Helton is Literary Arts Director for Hindman Settlement School in Knott County where she develops literature and creative writing programming for youth and the community. Her poetry and reviews have appeared in *Shenandoah, Anthology of Appalachian Writers, Still: The Journal, Norwegian Writers Climate Campaign* and more. Her chapbooks include *Inertia: A Study* (2016) and *Hewn* (2021). She has been awarded grants from Kentucky Foundation for Women as well as various prizes for poetry and essay. Originally from Toledo, Ohio, she has called eastern Kentucky home since 2010.

Jason Kyle Howard is editor of *Appalachian Review*. He is the author of *A Few Honest Words: The Kentucky Roots of Popular Music* and coauthor of *Something's Rising: Appalachians Fighting Mountaintop Removal.* His work has appeared in the *New York Times, the Atlantic, the Oxford American, Salon, the Nation, the Millions, Utne Reader,* and on NPR.

Dinamarie Isola is actively engaged in exploring the craft of storytelling. Through poetry and prose, she strives to tear down the isolation that comes from silently bearing internal struggles. She received her BA in English/Writing and Communications from Fairfield University. Her work has been published or is forthcoming in *A Thin Slice of Anxiety, Apricity Magazine, Avalon Literary Review, borrowed solace, Coachella Review, Courtship of Winds, Evening Street Review, Five on the Fifth, Mixed Mag, Nixes Mate Review, No Distance Between Us, Penumbra Literary and Art Journal, Potato Soup Journal, Remington Review*, and *Tulsa Review.*

Dan Leach has published poetry and short fiction in *Copper Nickel, The New Orleans Review, The Sun,* and *Appalachian Review.* He lives in South Carolina and teaches English at a small liberal arts university. He holds an MFA from Warren Wilson.

Elan Maier grew up in the San Francisco Bay area. As an actor in Chicago, he worked with Steppenwolf and the Goodman Theatre. He is a creative writing masters student at Oxford University (class of 2023) and is currently working on *Saint Piper Sand,* his first novel.

Jake Maynard is a fiction writer and essayist from McKean County, Pennsylvania. His work appears in *Southern Review, Guernica, Catapult, Slate, The New Republic, The New York Times,* and other publications. His debut novel, *Slime Line,* will be published in 2024 by West Virginia University Press. He lives in the kingdom of Pittsburgh.

A Virginia native, **Hayley Phillips** is now a PhD student at Louisiana State University and she received her MFA from Randolph College in 2021. Her work has been included or is forthcoming in *New Note Poetry, Beltway Quarterly,* and *Whale Road Review.* She currently lives in Baton Rouge with her husband and two dogs.

Kirsten Reneau received her MFA in creative nonfiction from the University of New Orleans. Her work has been featured in *The Threepenny Review, Hippocampus Magazine, Pine Mountain Sand & Gravel,* and other publications. Her chapbooks *Love Letters to the Heavens We Could Be In* and *Meeting Gods in Basement Bars and Other Ways to Find Forgiveness* are forthcoming in 2023.

www.ingramcontent.com/pod-product-compliance
Lightning Source LLC
Chambersburg PA
CBHW070604180626
46817CB00005B/1994